Creation of the Modern Middle East

The Kurds

Creation of the Modern Middle East

The Kurds

Heather Lehr Wagner

Introduction by
Akbar Ahmed
School of International Service
American University

CHELSEA HOUSE
P U B L I S H E R S
A Haights Cross Communications ◆— Company
Philadelphia

Frontispiece: Kurdish Woman and Child, Persia, c. 1920-21

CHELSEA HOUSE PUBLISHERS

EDITOR IN CHIEF Sally Cheney
DIRECTOR OF PRODUCTION Kim Shinners
CREATIVE MANAGER Takeshi Takahashi
MANUFACTURING MANAGER Diann Grasse

Staff for ᛐᚺᛖ ᚲᚢᚱᛞᛋ

EDITOR Lee Marcott
PRODUCTION ASSISTANT Jaimie Winkler
PICTURE RESEARCHER Sarah Bloom
COVER AND SERIES DESIGNER Keith Trego
LAYOUT 21st Century Publishing and Communications, Inc.

http://www.chelseahouse.com
A Haights Cross Communications ✦ Company

3 5 7 9 8 6 4 2

Library of Congress Cataloging-in-Publication Data

Wagner, Heather Lehr.
    The Kurds / Heather Lehr Wagner
            p. cm. -- (Creation of the modern Middle East)
Summary: A discussion of the people known as Kurds, including their
history as well as their contemporary status in the Middle East.
Includes bibliographical references and index.
    ISBN 0-7910-6505-7
1. Kurds--Middle East--Juvenile literature. [1.Kurds.] I. Title.
II.
Series.
    DS59.K86 W335 2002
    956'.00491597--dc21

                                                    2002009420

Table of Contents

Introduction by Akbar Ahmed   9

1   The Promise of a Homeland   19

2   A Tribal Society   35

3   The Kurds in Turkey   47

4   The Kurds in Iraq   69

5   The Kurds in Iran   93

6   Beyond the Gulf War   105

Gallery of Photographs of the Kurds   116

Appendix: The Treaty of Sèvres   130

Chronology   132

Further Reading   134

Bibliography   135

Index   136

Index to the Photographs

Kurdish Woman and Child, Persia, c. 1920-21   page 2

Modern Map of the Middle East   16

Kurdish Areas in the Middle East and
    the former Soviet Union   17

"Yusof, Bey of Koshk," c. 1893   18

Ottoman Cavalry Officers, Turkish Kurdistan, c. 1893-94   23

Kurd in Traditional Dress, Lake Van area, c. 1890s   24

Kurdish Woman, Eastern Turkey, 1894   26

Kurdish Village, Eastern Turkey, 1912   27

Kurdish Nomadic Camp, 1913   29

Kurd Village, Eastern Turkey, c. 1904-05   34

Azerbaijan Kurd, 1912   37

Kurdish Family, Isfahan Valley, Persia, c. 1912   39

Zahhak Kurds, c. 1902   42

Kurdish Aga, Lake Van area, 1894   44

The Kurdish Chief, c. 1906-09   46

Kurd, Shemsdinan District, Turkey, c. 1906-09   51

Ferryboat, Lake Van area, 1902   53

Mustafa Kemal Ataturk, 1932   57

Abdullah Ocalan, 1999   61

Refugee camp in Northern Iraq   65

Group of Iraqi Kurds, c. 1914   68

Young Kurdish Refugee Girl, 1991   70

Kurds, Turkish-Iraqi Border, 1919   73

Kurdish Tents, c. 1902   75

Iraqi Tribesmen with a Royal Air Force Officer, 1944   80

Kurdish Rebels Standing in the Ruins of a Village
    near Chami Razan, Iraq   86

Iran-Iraq War, 1980-85   89

Persian Kurds, 1912   92

Shah of Iran, Mohammad Reza Pahlavi, 1950   97

Ayatollah Ruhollah Khomeini, 1979   101

Jala Talabani, 2002   104

Iraqi Kurds, 1991   109

Turkish Kurds, 2001   111

Kurd Porters, Mount Ararat, c. 1893-94   118

Kalak, c. 1902   119

Armenian Soldiers, Eastern Turkey, c. 1906-09   120

Kurds, East of the Tigris River, c. 1906-09   121

Kurdish Sowars, Persia, c. 1908-09   122

Camel Caravan, 1912   123

Kurdish Father and Children, Isfahan Valley,
    Persia, c. 1912   124

Kurdish Musicians, Isfahan Valley, Persia, c. 1912   125

"Kurdish Robber Chiefs," 1912   126

Street Scene, Tabriz, 1912   127

Kurdish Village, 1913   128

Persian Kurd Plowing, c. 1920-21   129

Creation of the Modern Middle East

Iran

Iraq

Israel

Jordan

The Kurds

Kuwait

Oman

Palestinian Authority

Saudi Arabia

Syria

Turkey

Yemen

Introduction

Akbar Ahmed

The Middle East, it seems, is always in the news. Unfortunately, most of the news is of a troubling kind. Stories of suicide bombers, hijackers, street demonstrations, and ongoing violent conflict dominate these reports. The conflict draws in people living in lands far from the Middle East; some support one group, some support another, often on the basis of kinship or affinity and not on the merits of the case.

The Middle East is often identified with the Arabs. The region is seen as peopled by Arabs speaking Arabic and belonging to the Islamic faith. The stereotype of the Arab oil sheikh is a part of contemporary culture. But both of these images—that the Middle East is in perpetual anarchy and that it has an exclusive Arab identity—are oversimplifications of the region's complex contemporary reality.

In reality, the Middle East is an area that straddles Africa and Asia and has a combined population of over 200 million people inhabiting over twenty countries. It is a region that draws the entire world into its politics and, above all, it is the land that is the birth place of the three great Abrahamic faiths—Judaism, Christianity, and Islam. The city of Jerusalem is the point at which these three faiths come together and also where they tragically confront one another.

It is for these reasons that knowledge of the Middle East will remain of importance and that news from it will remain ongoing and interesting.

Let us consider the stereotype of the Middle East as a land of constant anarchy. It is easy to forget that some of the greatest lawgivers and people of peace were born, lived, and died here. In the Abrahamic tradition these names are a glorious roll call of human history—Abraham, Moses, Jesus, and Muhammad. In the tradition of the Middle East, where these names are especially revered, people often add the blessing "Peace be upon him" when speaking their names.

The land is clearly one that is shared by the great faiths. While it has a dominant Muslim character because of the large Muslim population, its Jewish and Christian presence must not be underestimated. Indeed, it is the dynamics of the relationships between the three faiths that allow us to enter the Middle East today and appreciate the points where these faiths come together or are in conflict.

To understand the predicament in which the people of the Middle East find themselves today, it is well to keep the facts of history before us. History is never far from the minds of the people in this region. Memories of the first great Arab dynasty, the Umayyads (661-750), based in Damascus, and the even greater one of the Abbasids (750-1258), based in Baghdad, are still kept alive in books and folklore. For the Arabs, their history, their culture, their tradition, their language, and above all their religion, provide them with a rich source of pride; but the glory of the past contrasts with the reality and powerlessness of contemporary life.

Many Arabs have blamed past rulers for their current situation beginning with the Ottomans who ruled them until World War I and then the European powers that divided their lands. When they achieved independence after World War II they discovered that the artificial boundaries created by the European powers cut across tribes and clans. Today, too, they complain that a form of Western imperialism still dominates their politics and rulers.

Again, while it is true that Arab history and Arab temperament have colored the Middle East strongly, there are other distinct peoples who have made a significant contribution to the culture of the region. Turkey is one such non-Arab nation with its own language, culture, and contribution to the region through the influence of the Ottoman Empire. Memories of that period for the Arabs are mixed, but what cannot be denied are the spectacular administrative and architectural achievements of the Ottomans. It is the longest dynasty in world history, beginning in 1300 and ending after World War I in 1922, when Kemal Ataturk wished to reject the past on the way to creating a modern Turkey.

Similarly, Iran is another non-Arab country with its own rich language and culture. Based in the minority sect of Islam, the Shia, Iran has often been in opposition to its Sunni neighbors, both Arab and Turk. Perhaps this confrontation helped to forge a unique Iranian, or Persian, cultural identity that, in turn, created the brilliant art, architecture, and poetry under the Safawids (1501-1722). The Safawid period also saw the establishment of the principle of interference or participation—depending on one's perspective—in matters of the state by the religious clerics. So while the Ayatollah Khomeini was very much a late 20th century figure, he was nonetheless reflecting the patterns of Iranian history.

Israel, too, represents an ancient, non-Arabic, cultural and religious tradition. Indeed, its very name is linked to the tribes that figure prominently in the stories of the Bible and it is through Jewish tradition that memory of the great biblical patriarchs like Abraham and Moses is kept alive. History is not a matter of years, but of millennia, in the Middle East.

Perhaps nothing has evoked as much emotional and political controversy among the Arabs as the creation of the state of Israel in 1948. With it came ideas of democracy and modern culture that seemed alien to many Arabs. Many saw the wars that followed stir further conflict and hatred; they also saw the wars as an inevitable clash between Islam and Judaism.

It is therefore important to make a comment on Islam and Judaism. The roots of prejudice against Jews can be anti-Semitic, anti-Judaic, and anti-Zionist. The prejudice may combine all three and there is often a degree of overlap. But in the case of the Arabs, the matter is more complicated because, by definition, Arabs cannot be anti-Semitic because they themselves are considered Semites. They cannot be anti-Judaic, because Islam recognizes the Jews as "people of the Book."

What this leaves us with is the clash between the political philosophy of Zionism, which is the establishment of a Jewish nation in Palestine, and Arab thought. The antagonism of the Arabs to Israel may result in the blurring of lines. A way must be found by Arabs and Israelis to live side by side in peace. Perhaps recognition of the common Abrahamic tradition is one way forward.

The hostility to Israel partly explains the negative coverage the Arabs get in the Western media. Arab Muslims are often accused of being anarchic and barbaric due to the violence of the Middle East. Yet, their history has produced some of the greatest figures in history.

Consider the example of Sultan Salahuddin Ayyoubi, popularly called Saladin in Western literature. Saladin had vowed to take revenge for the bloody massacres that the Crusaders had indulged in when they took Jerusalem in 1099. According to a European eyewitness account the blood in the streets was so deep that it came up to the knees of the horsemen.

Yet, when Saladin took Jerusalem in 1187, he showed the essential compassion and tolerance that is at the heart of the Abrahamic faiths. He not only released the prisoners after ransom, as was the custom, but paid for those who were too poor to afford any ransom. His nobles and commanders were furious that he had not taken a bloody revenge. Saladin is still remembered in the bazaars and villages as a leader of great learning and compassion. When contemporary leaders are compared to Saladin, they are usually found wanting. One reason may be that the problems of the region are daunting.

The Middle East faces three major problems that will need solutions in the twenty-first century. These problems affect society and politics and need to be tackled by the rulers in those lands and all other people interested in creating a degree of dialogue and participation.

The first of the problems is that of democracy. Although democracy is practiced in some form in a number of the Arab countries, for the majority of ordinary people there is little sense of participation in their government. The frustration of helplessness in the face of an indifferent bureaucracy at the lower levels of administration is easily converted to violence. The indifference of the state to the pressing needs of the "street" means that other non-governmental organizations can step in. Islamic organizations offering health and education programs to people in the shantytowns and villages have therefore emerged and flourished over the last decades.

The lack of democracy also means that the ruler becomes remote and autocratic over time as he consolidates his power. It is not uncommon for many rulers in the Middle East to pass on their rule to their son. Dynastic rule, whether kingly or based in a dictatorship, excludes ordinary people from a sense of participation in their own governance. They need to feel empowered. Muslims need to feel that they are able to participate in the process of government. They must feel that they are able to elect their leaders into office and if these leaders do not deliver on their promises, that they can throw them out. Too many of the rulers are nasty and brutish. Too many Muslim leaders are kings and military dictators. Many of them ensure that their sons or relatives stay on to perpetuate their dynastic rule.

With democracy, Muslim peoples will be able to better bridge the gaps that are widening between the rich and the poor. The sight of palatial mansions with security guards carrying automatic weapons standing outside them and, alongside, hovels teeming with starkly poor children is a common one in Muslim cities. The distribution of wealth must remain a priority of any democratic government.

The second problem in the Middle East that has wide ramifications in society is that of education. Although Islam emphasizes knowledge and learning, the sad reality is that the standards of education are unsatisfactory. In addition, the climate for scholarship and intellectual activity is discouraging. Scholars are too often silenced, jailed, or chased out of the country by the administration. The sycophants and the intelligence services whose only aim is to tell the ruler what he would like to hear, fill the vacuum.

Education needs to be vigorously reformed. The *madrassah,* or religious school, which is the institution that provides primary education for millions of boys in the Middle East, needs to be brought into line with the more prestigious Westernized schools reserved for the elite of the land. By allowing two distinct streams of education to develop, Muslim nations are encouraging the growth of two separate societies: a largely illiterate and frustrated population that is susceptible to leaders with simple answers to the world's problems and a small, Westernized, often corrupt and usually uncaring group of elite. The third problem facing the Middle East is that of representation in the mass media. Although this point is hard to pin down, the images in the media are creating problems of understanding and communication in the communities living in the Middle East. Muslims, for example, will always complain that they are depicted in negative stereotypes in the non-Arab media. The result of the media onslaught that plagues Muslims is the sense of anger on the one hand and the feeling of loss of dignity on the other. Few Muslims will discuss the media rationally. Greater Muslim participation in the media and greater interaction will help to solve the problem. But it is not so simple. The Israelis also complain of the stereotypes in the Arab media that depict them negatively.

Muslims are aware that their religious culture represents a civilization rich in compassion and tolerance. They are aware that given a period of stability in which they can grapple with the problems of democracy, education, and self-image they can take their rightful place in the community of nations. However painful the current reality, they do carry an idea of an ideal human society with them. Whether a Turk, or an Iranian, or an Arab, every Muslim is aware of the message that the prophet of Islam brought to this region in the seventh century. This message still has resonance for these societies. Here are words from the last address of the prophet spoken to his people:

> All of you descend from Adam and Adam was made of earth. There is no superiority for an Arab over a non-Arab nor for a non-Arab over an Arab, neither for a white man over a black man nor a black man over a white man . . . the noblest among you is the one who is most deeply conscious of God.

This is a noble and worthy message for the twenty-first century in the Middle East. Not only Muslims, but Jews, and Christians would agree with it. Perhaps its essential theme of tolerance, compassion, and equality can help to rediscover the wellsprings of tradition that can both inspire and unite.

It is for these reasons that I congratulate Chelsea House Publishers for taking the initiative in helping us to understand the Middle East through this series. The story of the Middle East is, in many profound ways, the story of human civilization.

— **Dr. Akbar S. Ahmed**
The Ibn Khaldun Chair of Islamic Studies and
Professor of International Relations,
School of International Service
American University

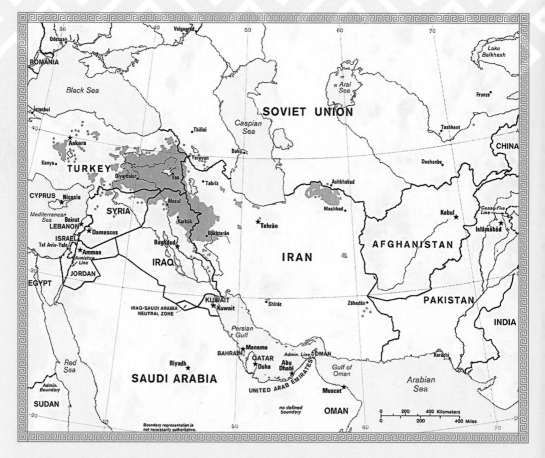

Kurdish Areas in the Middle East and the former Soviet Union

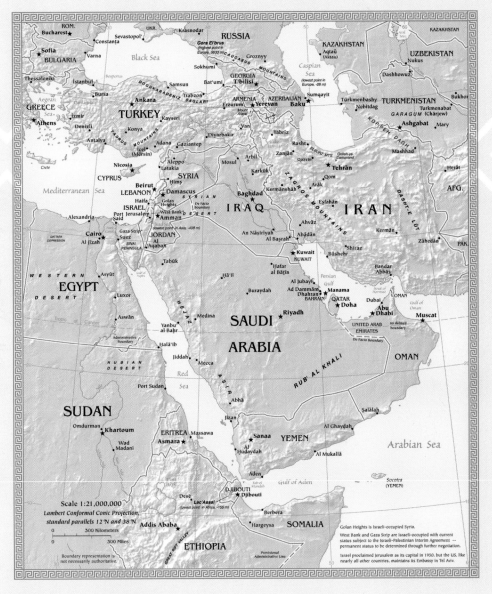

Modern Map of the Middle East

"Yusof, Bey of Koshk," c. 1893

Under the Ottoman Empire, a *bey* was a governor of a province. The Ottomans have been accused of many things, but administration of their diverse empire must rank among their achievements. This Kurdish bey is an example of how the Ottoman Empire incorporated local ethnic leaders into their complex administrative system.

1

The Promise
of a Homeland

t was late in October 1918, and British officers based in Baghdad were nervous. World War I had ended, and Britain and its fellow members of the Allied forces had been victorious. The mighty Ottoman Empire, which had fought against the Allies so fiercely in Mesopotamia, had been defeated, and now British ships patrolled the Bosphorus River and British, French, Italian, and Greek troops freely occupied nearly two-thirds of the Ottoman territory.

Two years earlier, foreign ministers from Britain and France had signed a treaty that spelled out their plans to carve up the parts of the Ottoman Empire that stretched across the land we know today as the Middle East. This treaty, known as the Sykes-Picot

Agreement, was ratified by Russia a few months after Britain and France approved it. As its part of the post-war territory, Russia was granted the land known as Kurdistan, a region set in the heart of the Empire, overlapping territories that we know today as Turkey, Iraq, and Iran. But in that early part of the 20th century, those countries did not exist as independent nations. They were all part of the vast Ottoman Empire, an Empire that was now being sliced apart in the war's aftermath.

Russia's possession of Kurdistan did not last long. In the post-war chaos, revolution struck Russia, and the tsarist monarchy fell to the Soviet independence movement. Struggling to set up a new, communist system of government, the Soviets had little interest in expanding their empire by seizing land from neighboring countries, and so the fate of Kurdistan swung back to rest in the hands of Britain and France.

As those nations met to decide the future of the Middle East, freedom and justice for the native people were far from their mind. They had fought the Ottoman armies in fierce and often bloody combat. Now, with victory firmly in their grasp, humanitarian concerns were not uppermost in their thoughts. Instead, the British and French officials were focused on strategic goals—in breaking up the Ottoman Empire and setting up governments friendly to their own interests.

When Soviet Russia announced, on December 3, 1917, that it did not recognize any of the agreements the Tsar's government had signed relating to the Ottoman Empire, the other Allied nations quickly stepped in to seize the land granted to Russia. The United States, having participated in the Allied victory, was quite interested in taking advantage of this opening. U.S. representatives suggested setting up an Armenian state in much of the territory that was to have gone to Russia, setting up a Turkish state in part of

Anatolia with Istanbul as its capital, and then creating a Kurdish state out of what remained—essentially one-fourth of what had been Kurdistan. All of this, of course, would be placed under U.S. administration.

But British officials in the region had their eyes on this particular prize for their own country. And they had the advantage of already being the largest occupying force in the region. A mere four days after the end of the war, British forces had rushed into the Vilayet (province) of Mosul, in a part of Kurdistan that the Sykes-Picot Agreement had designated for France. There was one clear reason for their rush to claim this land for Britain—it was full of oil.

IN SEARCH OF AN ALLY

As 1918 drew to a close, British officials in the region decided that the best way to control Kurdistan would be to find an ally and make him the Kurdish leader. With a friendly face in charge of Kurdish affairs, Britain was confident of its ability to dominate the region and control its valuable oil resources. But the candidates for leader of the Kurds were few, and each presented a different set of problems.

On the short list of possible Kurdish leaders was Shaykh Abd al Qadir. Abd al Qadir was the second son of one of the most powerful spiritual leaders in Kurdistan. His older brother had inherited their father's wealth and power in the region, leaving Abd al Qadir feeling resentful and bored. He had been involved in the Committee of Union and Progress (C.U.P.), the political party that had helped overthrow the Ottoman Empire's ruler, and more recently had helped create the Kurdish Club, a group of upper-class Kurds interested in setting up an independent state for Kurdistan. While the group had been founded by wealthy noblemen, it had more recently attracted support from a number of local tribes and villagers, and had branches in several different towns.

But Abd al Qadir had been living in Istanbul—the capital of the Ottoman Empire—not Kurdistan. His ties were much closer to the cosmopolitan, urban, upper class of Istanbul than to his more rural countrymen in Kurdistan. While he had many wealthy supporters in Istanbul, the British were not confident that he would actually be able to win the support of the people he would ultimately be governing.

Another candidate under British consideration was General Sharif Pasha. Active in the Kurdish party since 1908, Sharif Pasha had, unfortunately, been living in exile for many years in France, banished for his suspected involvement in a plot to overthrow the Ottoman monarch. While he spoke confidently about the future of Kurdistan and the dangers it faced from Turkish forces, he did so from the comfort and security of his plush Paris apartment. By May of 1919, Sharif Pasha was putting out feelers to British officials through their embassy in Paris, indicating that he would be willing to take on the "burden" of ruling over an independent Kurdistan, but once more the British wondered whether the people would rally around someone who had lived abroad, safely removed from their day-to-day struggle, for so many years.

One other candidate for the job was Shaykh Taha, the nephew of Abd al Qadir and an intelligent young man who had been imprisoned by Russia during the war and only recently released. Taha had been actively campaigning for the job of Kurdish leader, suggesting to British authorities that all of Kurdistan should be united and that he was the man to do it. Taha's motives were even more far-reaching—he wanted to increase the amount of

Ottoman Cavalry Officers, Turkish Kurdistan, c. 1893-94

Under the Ottoman Empire, the military institution (*seyfive*) was responsible for expanding and defending the Empire and keeping order and security within the sultan's dominions.

Kurdish land to include part of Iran, and asked Britain to give him the weapons to do it. But Britain refused to hand over the needed rifles, and when Taha learned that Britain was also considering his uncle for the role of Kurdish leader, he quickly turned, pledging his loyalty to the Turks instead.

Kurd in Traditional Dress, Lake Van area, c. 1890s

The traditional Kurdish way of life was nomadic, revolving around sheep and goat herding throughout the Mesopotamian plains and the highlands of Turkey and Iran. Note the cartridge belt around the man's waist.

As different candidates were considered and rejected, different loyalties were exposed and put down. Had the Kurds been united, had a strong leader risen to power, the modern Middle East might have a very different geography. But instead, the climate of competition left chaos, splitting Kurds into those who supported Turkish forces, those who supported greater Allied involvement in the region, and those who wanted complete independence. And no one group fell squarely into one of these three categories—each kept hedging its bets, depending on who was making the best offer at any particular moment.

THE TREATY OF SÈVRES

In August of 1920, the victorious Allied powers gathered in France to divide the Middle East. Actively participating in the conference were Britain, France, Italy, Japan, Armenia, Belgium, Greece, Hedjaz (which we know today as Saudi Arabia), Poland, Portugal, Romania, the Serb-Croat-Slovene state (which would later become Yugoslavia, and still later split again into separate regions), Czechoslovakia, and Turkey. The United States and a Kurdish delegation attended, but only as observers. After intense debate, the conference concluded on August 10 with the signing of a lengthy treaty, containing 433 points, or articles.

Article 62 dealt specifically with the fate of Kurdistan. It indicated that the Allied powers would prepare for a self-governing territory "in those regions where the Kurdish element is preponderant lying east of the Euphrates, to the south of a still-to-be established Armenian frontier and to the north of the frontier between Turkey, Syria, and Mesopotamia." The treaty went on to state that if, within one year of the treaty's going into effect, the majority of the people living in that territory wished to become fully

Kurdish Woman, Eastern Turkey, 1894

independent of Turkey, then Turkey agreed to renounce all rights to the region.

The Kurds were clearly offered the promise of independence, of their own Kurdish state. And yet what they were being offered was, essentially, less than half a country.

Kurdish Village, Eastern Turkey, 1912

The Kurds—thought to number about 15 million today—live in contiguous areas of Iran, Iraq, and Turkey, a region generally referred to as Kurdistan although only Iran recognizes an area with that name.

Traditional Kurdish life was nomadic revolving around the raising of goats and sheep. However, the enforcement of national boundaries after World War I (1914-18) forced most Kurds to settle in villages.

At the Paris Peace Conference (1919), Kurdish nationalists appealed to U.S. President Woodrow Wilson for an independent Kurdistan. He agreed. The Treaty of Sèvres (1920) provided for such a nation—but the treaty was never ratified because of the opposition of Atatürk and his supporters. The Treaty of Lausanne (1923) replaced Sèvres, but it made no mention of Kurdistan or the Kurds. Indeed, Kurdistan was now more fragmented than before the war.

Under Atatürk's rule (1923-38), the Turkish Kurds were deprived of their national identity. Their official designation became "Mountain Turks" and their language was classified as a Turkish dialect. Kurds were forbidden to wear their distinctive costume.

But Kurdish nationalism only intensified. As recently as 1996, the European Tariff Union delayed Turkey's entry because of its continued harsh treatment of the Kurds. Members of human rights groups publicized the atrocities—the destruction of Kurdish towns by Turkish military forces and the persecution of Kurdish leaders. Although some U. S. officials questioned the purchase of military equipment by Turkey, which could be used to bomb Kurdish villages, no action was taken to halt such sales.

Much of the traditional Kurdish land lay west of the Euphrates River, a region that was to be handed over to France. The oil-rich region of Mosul was not included either—its people would be offered the opportunity to vote on whether or not to join Kurdistan only after it had become an official state and only if the Allied powers determined that the citizens of Mosul were capable of making that choice. The independent Kurdistan the Kurds were being promised was only one-third of the territory they hoped to receive. Missing were the most fertile regions, the grazing grounds and valuable parts of Persia (present-day Iran). All that remained were the poorest regions in the center of what had once been Kurdistan, surrounded by territories controlled by France in the west, Syria in the south, Persia in the east, and Armenia in the north. Britain would control the oil in the region.

It was a disappointing deal. And even that would be denied them. For as the Ottoman Empire crumbled and broke into pieces, the Kurds would be left without a homeland. As other nations formed and grew, the Kurds would be left to carve out a living in other peoples' countries, unwanted residents of Turkey, Iraq, Iran, and Syria. Their chance for independence began and, in a sense, ended with the signing of the Treaty of Sèvres. But their quest for freedom and a land of their own continues to this day.

THE FALL OF AN EMPIRE

As early as the 13th century, there was a territory in the Middle East described as "Kurdistan." Its people, known as Kurds, were primarily nomads, moving from higher lands in the summer to lower ground during colder weather. They survived by trading goods, and when the Mongols swept into the region to form the beginnings of the Ottoman Empire, the Kurds built a relationship with

Kurdish Nomadic Camp, 1913

A nomad is a person who has no fixed home but rather moves from place to place in search of food or pasture land. This photograph shows a typical Kurdish nomadic encampment.

them based on trade and offers of security. The Ottomans created 15 small regions, known as *emirates*, and set up Kurdish leaders to administer them in a way friendly to Ottoman interests.

At its peak, in the 1500s and 1600s, the Ottoman Empire contained as much land as the continental United States, stretching out into Asia, parts of Europe and northern

Africa, and the countries known today as Turkey, Iran, Saudi Arabia, Iraq, and Syria. But as the 19th century drew to a close, the Empire was crumbling. The power of sultans, the spiritual and political monarchs that ruled over the vast territory, was weakening as they grew more corrupt, and rumblings of discontent were growing louder. Certain regions of the Empire, particularly the Balkans, were reaching out for independence, and the Ottomans determined to hold on to their Empire by stamping out any local competition for power.

The emirates tried to fight back, but their attempts at revolt and the earliest hints of a Kurdish independence movement were unsuccessful. The Ottomans destroyed the emirates, but the discontent was spreading, from the farthest regions of the Empire to its very capital.

As the 1800s drew to a close, the streets of Istanbul, the capital city, were full of plotters, young men who were tired of the corruption of the wealthy monarchs and of having opportunities denied to them. The once glittering seaport showed signs of wear, an omen to those dreaming of revolution that the time might be right to strike for independence. The C.U.P. was born in a climate of dissatisfaction and disorder—a forum for many who were seeking an outlet for their ambitions through political activities. The members of this new and secret party, many of whom came from the army, swore loyalty to only two things: the Koran (the holy book of the Islamic faith) and the gun. Their plans were for a new order, a new society freed from the corrupt traditions that were—in their view—weakening the Ottoman Empire. They did not want a true revolution; they merely wanted to restore the empire to its former glory.

A visitor to Istanbul at the beginning of the 20th century would have found a city whose days of glory seemed far behind it. The capital of the Ottoman Empire had served as a setting for so many of the greatest civilizations the world had known. The Hittites had dominated the region during the Middle Bronze Age, fighting Egyptian pharaohs and battling the Greeks until losing the land to the Persians. Alexander the Great conquered the land around 300 B.C., and later came the mighty Roman Empire. The ancient city of Byzantium was rebuilt under Constantine in 300 A.D., and as the new capital city, it became known as Constantinople. An entire empire—the Byzantine Empire—spread out from this city into Asia and the Balkan Peninsula. Later, conquering Islamic dynasties moved from Mecca into the region.

By 1453, a new group had swept into Constantinople: nomadic tribesmen known as the Ottoman Turks. Fierce warriors on horseback, they traveled across the lands, seizing territory as they headed west across Asia and on into Europe. Setting their capital in the same glittering setting that Constantine had chosen, the Ottomans created an empire that was the most powerful in the world.

But gradually, their territories slipped away. Corruption dominated the government. The sultans who ruled the empire frequently seized the throne from family members, either by murdering them or by locking them away. Citizens of the empire were divided into two general classes, or groups. The upper class, which included the imperial family, wealthy landowners and religious and military leaders, paid no taxes. The lower class, consisting mainly of peasants, farmers and some craftsmen, paid taxes to support the lavish lifestyles of their rulers.

The oppressive taxes, the frequently weak sultans, the corruption and bribery that marked the military, all contributed to the loss of greatness. By the beginning of the 20th century, important territories such as Greece and Egypt had been lost. With each loss of territory, large groups of Muslim refugees would come pouring into the remains of the empire. Rumblings of independence, first having touched the people in the farthest stretches of the empire, now echoed in the streets of the capital city.

AN IDENTITY CRISIS

As the seeds of discontent spread throughout the Ottoman Empire, a radical change was happening in the hearts and minds of its people. Where once they had considered themselves Ottomans, an identity that indicated a certain sophistication and cosmopolitan glamour, they now began to view themselves in different terms. As pieces of the Empire crumbled away, the Empire no longer assumed the face of a benevolent monarch but, increasingly, began to seem like a corrupt and oppressive occupying force. As dissatisfaction with the monarch and his government grew, the young revolutionaries were less willing to identify themselves as Ottoman citizens. Instead they sought a different, more progressive label, and for many this was based on their home territory.

When the revolution came, in 1908, many upper-class Kurds were quick to join the movement sparked by the C.U.P. A number of Kurdish political journals, such as *Hitavi Kurd* (Kurdish Sun) and *Kurt Teavun we Taraki Gazetesi* (Kurdish Mutual Aid and Progress Gazette), were published, and Kurdish political groups like the Kurdish Club and the Kurdish Hope Society grew in numbers. It was a time for residents or former residents from the Kurdish territory to join other politically motivated young men in shaping a new destiny for the Ottoman Empire.

But their time in the political spotlight would not last long. The C.U.P. had as its core aim to restore the Ottoman Empire to its former glory, to end the era of the corrupt monarchy but not of the Empire itself. They sensed that those who were beginning to capitalize on their ethnic identity could mean a further breakdown in the political system as different groups sought their own power bases. By August of 1909, a law had been passed banning political groups that were based on ethnic identities. Many of those who had formed Kurdish societies or produced Kurdish papers and journals were sent into exile, accused of revolutionary activity.

But the majority of the Kurdish politicians sent into exile had been guilty only of nationalism, not efforts to spark Kurdish independence. Their dreams of secession, of a separate Kurdish state, would come later, after years living away from their homeland and subtle encouragement from British officials anxious to build a friendly base in the region. But their dreams would be dashed. For only a brief moment in time, Kurdistan existed on paper as a separate nation. But its people would spend the next century like their nomadic forefathers, temporary citizens of unfriendly governments, waiting for a nation of their own.

Kurd Village, Eastern Turkey, c. 1904-05

It appears as if most of the males of the Kurdish village posed for this photograph. The photographer, H.E. Wilkie Young, served as a British Consul at Smyrna, which is present-day Izmir.

2

A Tribal Society

The story of the Kurds begins with a shattered dream. But while the Kurds were not able to attain their dream of a country of their own, they have continued to exist as a people, living within the borders of other countries. They continue to occupy a specific region within these countries. They have not assimilated (blended) into the people or culture around them, but instead have carved out their own separate community, a community defined as "Kurdish."

It is useful to understand the situation of the Kurds to better appreciate the modern Middle East, the still-evolving series of borders that separate nations in this strategically important region. But perhaps more importantly, the Kurds provide us with an

35

opportunity to think about the question of what truly constitutes a nation. Is it merely a series of solid lines on a map? Or is a nation more deeply defined as a collection of people sharing the same ethnic identity and seeking the same goals?

Today, there are about 27 million Kurds living in the Middle East. Approximately half of them live in Turkey, where they make up about 20 percent of the population. They also live in significant numbers in Iraq and Iran, and a smaller group live in Syria (generally along the Turkish frontier). Other communities of Kurds can be found in Europe, and in certain portions of the former Soviet republics. While they now are more widely scattered than they were at the beginning of the 20th century (in part as they fled oppression from the governments where they had been living), the heart of the Kurdish region remains where it was centuries earlier—the mountainous region that crosses over the borders of Iran, Iraq, and Turkey, the inter-section of those three nations.

In fact, it is this location that has, in part, contributed to the efforts of each country to control its Kurdish population and eliminate any potential problems. Each country has zealously guarded its strategic borders, with those moun-tains providing useful barriers to invading forces. The Kurdish independence movement threatened these governments at a point where they had no intent of becoming weak—their border. These countries have had numerous disputes, but they all are in agreement on one point: they have no intention of allowing the Kurds to carve out their own country.

Similarly, the Kurds have found themselves inhabitants of land rich with oil and water resources. Iraq, Turkey, and Syria rely heavily on the oilfields located in Kurdish territories; both Iraq and Turkey are similarly dependent on water flowing from Kurdish land. For the Kurds, this

Azerbaijan Kurd, 1912

This is a rare photograph of an Azerbaijan Kurd. He is carrying a native carpet. Azerbaijan is a region in the extreme northwest area of Persia (Iran).

blessing has become a curse, making it highly unlikely that countries dependent on the resources Kurdish land provides will willingly let it go.

But there is more to the story of the Kurds than simply the history of a people struggling against oppressive governments unwilling to grant them their freedom. Had the problem been so simple and straightforward, it is possible that the nation of Kurdistan would exist today. But it does not, and the answer lies as much in the behavior of the Kurds themselves as it does in the attitudes of the countries where they live.

A COMMON CULTURE?

The term Kurdistan has defined a specific region since the early 13th century, generally the land falling on either side of the Zagros Mountains where Iraq, Iran, and Turkey meet. It is a rugged and difficult land, cold in winter and hot and dry in summer. But there is no Kurdistan on modern maps, although there is a distinct culture and ethnic group that can be defined as "Kurdish."

Certainly the countries where the majorities of Kurds live (Turkey, Iran and Iraq) would be reluctant to admit that there is a separate region within their borders. Particularly in those countries where borders were defined through bloody battles and whose leaders have seized power following the violent overthrow of another system of government, there can be no challenge from a minority group, claiming a piece of land that rightfully belongs to another country.

In fact, it would be a mistake to assume that all Kurds, whether they are found in Turkey or Iraq, are essentially the same people. In many cases, they do not even speak the same language. Kurds living in the north generally speak a language known as Kurmanji, while those in the south speak in Surani.

Kurdish Family, Isfahan Valley, Persia, c. 1912

The Isfahan Valley, along the Zayandeh River, is located about 200 miles south of Tehran.

Iranian, or Persian, Kurds speak dialects that are closer to modern Persian than they are to the languages of their fellow Kurds.

The majority of all Kurds are Muslims, dating back to the 7th century when Arab invaders swept into the region. They are Sunni Muslims, but their belief system is based on the Shafi'i school of thought, rather than the Hanafi version that became more common when the Ottomans took over the region in the 16th century. The distinctions are subtle—to believers, Hanafi is more formal, while Shafi'i practices might be described as more "folk-like." In part, the explanation for this is geographical—lacking access to formal mosques and the teachings of conservative *mullahs* (spiritual instructors), constrained by the demands of a more rugged daily life, Kurds have gained a reputation for being less strict in following Islamic teachings and practices. But even within the Kurdish communities there are subtle differences in religious beliefs, as well as smaller communities of Christians (including Assyrians and Armenians), Jews, and others.

As we can see, one of the overwhelming difficulties facing the Kurds in their effort to build a nation has been internal—the differences separating one group of Kurds from another. This is not a recent development, explained away by the carving up of Kurdistan into different, autonomous countries. Instead, it dates back to the earliest days of Kurdish culture.

The Kurds were nomads, and their society was a tribal one. A *tribe* can be loosely defined as a group of people descended from a single ancestor who share the same customs and heritage. In Kurdish society, the tribes were frequently based on heritage, most often proudly tracing their family connections back to some significant figure in Islam. Tribes also had a regional connection—sharing a connection to a particular piece of land that they might have traditionally farmed or used to raise livestock.

Much of Kurdish identity prior to the 20th century came from connections to their tribe, rather than to a larger state or authority. Most Kurds would not have described themselves using that term, but would instead have referred to themselves based on their tribe or religious group.

The difficulty in uniting a people who believed they had little in common with each other explains, at least in part, why the Kurdish struggle for independence has remained just that—a struggle. Urban Kurds had no interest in identifying themselves with more rural, even peasant-class, Kurds. Rival tribes competed for power and control over a particular region. Even within a single tribe, power clashes took place to determine who would be in charge of a particular group, and alliances would form, break down, and reform each time the opportunity presented itself. Power struggles also took place between the *shaikhs*, the leaders of each religious community, and the *aghas*, the chiefs who controlled each small village or town. There were also communities of Kurds who were non-tribal, and they were generally looked down upon by tribal Kurds, who demanded labor from these non-tribal Kurds in exchange for protection from unfriendly invaders.

It is clear that Kurdish society was based in large part on regional, rather than national, control. Kurds tended to live in smaller communities, often based on ancient family connections. All of the residents in a Kurdish village might be related to each other, dating back centuries, and they all respected the authority of the local leaders who made decisions about everything from how food and water resources would be allocated to who could be married—and to whom. This kind of local control—following the authority of the local agha or shaikh—posed a challenge to those wanting to unite all Kurds in the struggle to obtain their own homeland in the early part of the 20th century. The local leaders were not interested in ceding their power to a greater, national authority. The Kurds identified themselves not as "Kurds," but rather as members of this tribe, or this religious group. They saw no need for a revolution.

The mountains that they occupied sheltered them from the changes that swept across the Middle East at the beginning of the 20th century. By the time they realized

Zahhak Kurds, c. 1902

The Zahhak Kurds believe they are descended from the forefathers of the Kurds. In this photograph, the three men are standing on the ruins of an ancient Syrian Christian church.

how much the world had changed, and what it would mean for them, it was too late.

THE GOLDEN AGE OF KURDISTAN

For a people who have often been criticized for not being truly devout Muslims, it is interesting to note that the Kurds first began to flourish with the arrival of Islam to the region. As the Kurds converted to the new faith, they were welcomed by the *caliph*, the leader of the faith, who valued the Kurds' ability to fight fiercely and fearlessly. Kurds soon occupied leadership positions in the Islamic armies—in fact, one Kurd (known as Saladin) led the charge that re-conquered Jerusalem and the Holy Land from the Christian Crusaders, a victory that would transform the history of the region and result in religious conflict many centuries later.

For this brief period in time, Kurdistan enjoyed an age of military power and economic significance, but it would not last long. By the late 15th century, Ottoman Turks had swept into the region and busily built an empire, conquering lands and blocking European efforts to expand to the east. Blocked off from their trade routes to the east, Europeans determined to head west, leading them to ultimately settle a new continent.

But for the Kurds, whose economy had been based in part on collecting tolls from their location squarely along the trade routes, whose villages had supplied traders with goods necessary for their journey, the outcome was much less fortunate. Gradually, economies withered away and once-prosperous towns now needed to carve out a new living from the rough land—a living based on tending livestock and farming crops like tobacco and cotton.

The fierce fighting skills of the Kurds, skills that had once made them valued military generals, also made them dangerous enemies. The Ottomans were undecided about how best to ensure that these warriors did not become revolutionaries. A system of local government was set up, with regions either administered by local governments or by an *emir* or royal ruler selected by the Ottomans.

By the 19th century, the Ottoman Empire was beginning to decline. The decline was felt in the more far-flung

Kurdish Aga, Lake Van area, 1894

This Kurdish *aga* (right) is photographed with his servant and ram. Under the Ottoman Empire, an aga was a person of high rank or social position.

corners of the empire first, as Ottoman authority began to fade. The emirs decided to do something about it, taking advantage of the absence of Ottoman authority to set up their own mini-kingdoms.

Many experts feel that this decline shaped the lack of unity that would one day make it impossible for Kurds to unify sufficiently to claim their own homeland. Emirs would quarrel with each other over power and territory. The Ottomans had frequently selected weak rulers deliberately so that they would not present a challenge to the central authority. Left to their own devices, these weak rulers frequently relied more and more heavily on oppressive taxes to administer their kingdoms. Violence was common; criminal behavior and corruption even more so.

Gradually, the clock began to turn backwards for the

Kurds. In other parts of the Ottoman Empire, urban life and exposure to Western culture began to shape the thinking that would lead to nationalism. But in Kurdistan, authority began to rest more and more heavily in the hands of the aghas—the tribal chiefs. Recognizable authority existed most clearly on the local level.

For a brief time, the Kurds occupied positions of power, recognized and valued for their contributions by the leaders of their faith. But that era had passed by the time revolution came to the Ottoman Empire. The Kurds would fight for freedom, joining the C.U.P. in overthrowing a corrupt regime, believing that the result would be a new age in which they would play a crucial role. But they were deceived. A new kind of leadership was rising from the ashes of the Ottoman Empire. And it would view the Kurdish people not as an ally, but as a threat.

The Kurdish Chief, c. 1906-09

This Kurdish chief, seated on the white horse, is surrounded by his armed guards.

   The Young Turk Revolution (1908) resulted in a constitution for the Ottoman Empire. However, almost immediately, the Young Turks adopted repressive policies against non-Turkish people, especially the Armenians and the Kurds. Kurdish organizations and publications were outlawed.

3

The Kurds
in Turkey

On July 24, 1923, the Treaty of Lausanne was signed—a very different document from the Treaty of Sèvres that carried the promise of a land for the Kurds. This document would set in motion the events that would ensure that a separate Kurdish homeland would not exist. For the Treaty of Lausanne spelled out many of the ways in which the remnants of the Ottoman Empire would be transformed into the modern state of Turkey. And that new state would rise as a result of the activities of a new group of nationalists, led by Mustafa Kemal.

During World War I, Mustafa Kemal had served his country brilliantly, particularly in the decisive battle at Gallipoli. But in the aftermath of the war, a new movement was sweeping through the

Middle East. In many quarters, lands long occupied by colonial forces were now eager to throw off the shackles of these frequently oppressive forms of government. They had fought long and hard to ensure freedom for other countries. Now they wanted their own freedom.

Mustafa Kemal successfully rallied a significant portion of the Turkish population to his cause of nationalism. And the Treaty of Lausanne proved a vindication of their efforts. Many of the military and political demands Mustafa and his fellow nationalists had made in the aftermath of World War I were granted in the treaty. More importantly, representatives from his nationalist cause (as well as representatives of the sultan who ruled the territory) were invited to the treaty signing.

The treaty proved the catalyst to propel Turkey onto the next stage of its development. It granted the land that now makes up all of modern Turkey to the new state. Mustafa had a clear vision for how the government of this new state would evolve. The first step had been achieved: spelling out the borders of this new nation. The next step was equally clear: eliminate the sultan.

Much of the nationalist cause centered on the concept of a unified, modern Turkey—a nation based on Western principles and a strong, central government. There would be economic and scientific efforts to ensure Turkey's place in the community of nations as an equal. It was a time for strong leadership, under a single leader with a clear vision. Mustafa was determined to be that leader.

Under the leadership of Mustafa Kemal, Turkey would undergo a radical, revolutionary transformation. From the beginning, the Turkey he envisioned would be a secular (non-religious) country. The *caliph*—the religious leader of Islam who had been based in Istanbul, Turkey's capital—was forced to leave the country. For the Kurds, who had derived the little power they held from their links to Islamic shaikhs and aghas, this transformation would mean the steady slipping away of any loss of status they might have held.

The next threat would come to their very definition as a people. Another key to Mustafa Kemal's transformation of Turkish society was to change the way people thought of themselves. No more were they to be defined by their religious status within the stratified Islamic society that had flourished in the Ottoman Empire. No more were they to think of themselves by their regional affiliation, nor as subjects in an empire. They were to become Turks, a proud people, governed as citizens of a republic. For the Kurds, this meant a loss not only of their limited Islamic status, but also of their cultural identity, of their reliance on local government and local systems of administration—a threat to the way of life they had experienced for centuries.

The modern society that Kemal envisioned rapidly became a reality, and it is difficult to imagine how quickly life changed for his people. For Kemal, this accomplishment was born of political and personal necessity. He wanted to ensure that no more pieces of Turkey pulled away, as they had under Ottoman rule. He wanted to unite his people as never before. And he wanted to be a leader of a great nation.

Pulling a nation back from the threat of political destruction is a brilliant feat; changing the way its people think about themselves and their culture is almost impossible. And yet Kemal was able to achieve both. Soon people were required to wear Western-style clothing. Women were encouraged to abandon the practice of wearing the veil, and to take a more active role in Turkish society. Kemal changed the way his people measured time, introducing the Christian calendar and the 24-hour system of measuring time that was in use in Europe. He changed the way Turks wrote, outlawing the use of the Arabic alphabet.

Ultimately, he so completely changed the identity of Turks that he was able to require them to take a new name. He himself changed his own name, to one more befitting the leader of this thriving republic. He renamed himself Atatürk, meaning "Father Turk."

While Atatürk viewed himself as the "father of all Turks," it was a family whose members did not all uniformly support his autocratic rule. The changes that modernized and Westernized so much of Turkey came at a high price for the Kurds. Bit by bit, their very identity was being erased. It was part of Atatürk's vision that Turkey must stand united, with the nation being stronger and greater than any of its individual regions. But this form of national identity was alien to the Kurds. Many of them lived rural lives. They enjoyed few of the benefits of a more modern Turkey, but the restrictions and changes were felt particularly keenly. Their Kurdish schools, publications and societies were all closed. The authority of their local leaders—the aghas and shaikhs—was gradually eliminated.

It is not surprising that a rebellion soon broke out within Kurdish ranks. Many of the new Turkish policies were viewed as racist in their complete and absolute intolerance for any use of non-Turkish language and in their systematic elimination of a way of life that had survived for centuries. The Kurdish nationalist movement had flourished initially in more urban areas, among the upper-class Kurds, but as the impact of new Turkish policies spread out throughout all Kurdish territories, a new energy for Kurdish independence became evident. A group known as *Azadi* (Freedom) was established in 1923 and spread quickly, particularly among those Kurds serving in the Turkish armed forces, but also in the more rural areas.

The obstacles that had prevented the Kurds from

Kurd, Shemsdinan District, Turkey, c. 1906-09

The Shemsdinan District of eastern Turkey was noted for its wooded slopes and celebrated for its tobacco.

successfully negotiating their own homeland following World War I continued to haunt Azadi from the beginning. The basic structure of Kurdish life made it difficult to achieve the kind of coordination and effective communication needed to bring about any kind of revolt. In 1925, a group of prominent Kurds—mainly shaikhs and army officers—determined to fight for a free and independent Kurdistan. Rumors of a rebellion quickly reached the Turkish capital, and troops were sent to Kurdish areas to ensure that the revolt was quickly put down.

This initial effort revealed the weaknesses inherent in the Kurdish efforts. The rebels were unable to successfully coordinate local Kurds to join them. In many cases, it was their own fault. Urban Kurds looked down upon the peasants and farmers. Military Kurds deemed others "unfit" to fight. Tribal Kurds ignored the non-tribal Kurds, and as a result they lost the opportunity to add additional men to their fighting force.

It did not take long for Turkish forces to stamp out the rebellion, hang those involved or suspected of being involved, and take steps to ensure that additional rebellions did not break out. Martial law was declared in all of Kurdistan. Large numbers of Turkish soldiers were mobilized and moved to the southeast region where the revolts had begun.

ELIMINATING REBELLION

A new series of legal measures was passed that essentially authorized the use of any and all measures to eliminate Kurdish rebellion from spreading. The revolt had given Atatürk an excuse to take steps to wipe out any possible sources of rebellion in Kurdish territory. All Kurdish leaders who had acted or might in future act against the government were arrested and, in many cases, executed. But the suppression went further. Thousands of Kurds were deported

Ferryboat, Lake Van area, 1902

Lake Van, the largest body of water in Turkey, is located in eastern Anatolia, near the border with Iran.

from their homes, their villages destroyed, their leaders eliminated. By May of 1932, laws had been passed to evacuate certain Kurdish areas, particularly in Anatolia, and to encourage Turks to move into those regions and settle them. In villages where Kurds remained, they were kept under strict control. Martial law was enforced, the use of Kurdish language was forbidden. The use of Kurdish clothing or Kurdish names was outlawed. Any remaining Kurdish schools were closed. Cattle and livestock were taken away, effectively condemning much of the population to starve to death.

Atatürk had determined that the borders of Turkey were fixed, having been hard fought for and won. Turkey would be one nation, united in customs and costumes, language and lifestyle. There was no place for Kurdish rebellion. If the Kurds would not willingly contribute to the development of this new nation, they would suffer the consequences.

Thousands of refugees began to flee from Turkish Kurdistan, heading for what they hoped would be friendlier regimes in Iran, Iraq, and Syria. They carried with them horrifying tales of genocide, of entire villages destroyed, of concerted efforts to eliminate a people or, at the least, a way of life.

International pressure soon came to bear on the Turkish government. Much of the violence began to be scaled back, and a new phase of assimilation began, one perhaps less violent, but nonetheless designed to eliminate any sense of the Kurds as a separate population.

New efforts were launched to rebuild much of what had been destroyed in Turkey's eastern provinces. But those appointed to head up the reconstruction efforts were Turks. Positions of economic and political importance were given only to Turks. Efforts were made to eliminate the authority of the aghas—their large estates were broken into pieces and distributed to the peasants who had worked the land for centuries.

And a new campaign was launched, labeled the "Turkish Hearth Organization." This harmless-sounding group represented a systematic effort to wipe out any last vestiges of Islamic or ethnic thought by convincing everyone of the benefits of being Turkish. Representatives from the Turkish Hearth Organization were sent to Kurdistan, where they soon enjoyed great success among the middle- and upper-class Kurds, who understood that their future status in Turkey depended upon their willingness to become good Turks. Only those who could speak Turkish would get ahead. And the path to success led them away from their Kurdish provinces, where the only real jobs available were in the military or in farming.

Gradually, the educated and upwardly mobile Kurds began to leave their homeland, looking for greater opportunities elsewhere. The economy had never really recovered from its early losses at the beginning of the 20th century. Those who chose to stay, clinging to their Kurdish heritage, would fall behind.

TURKEY DIVIDED

The efforts to force all Kurds to become Turks entered a new and harsher stage in June of 1934. Atatürk's efforts to transform Turkish society had been successful. He enjoyed extensive support and loyalty from his people. With this, he was able to pass a new law, known as Law No. 2510, that divided his country into three zones:

- Zones for people who, it was felt, already possessed the necessary "Turkish culture";

- Zones where people of "non-Turkish culture" were to be moved in order to be successfully educated in Turkish language and customs;

- Zones that were to be completely evacuated.

It is clear that the goal of this law was to eliminate any significant Kurdish population from any region, by reducing the Kurdish population to no more than five percent in any given area. The government was granted the full authority to redistribute the citizens of Turkey as it saw fit. All property belonging to tribes or their leaders was subject to seizure by the government. Any remaining locales where Turkish was not spoken were to be eliminated.

It was an overwhelming example of the extent to which the Turkish government was willing to go to eradicate any last vestiges of Kurdish society. Only the real difficulties of forcibly moving more than three million people prevented the policy from being completely carried out. But estimates indicate that approximately one million Kurds were displaced, and many more young men were forcibly drafted into the Turkish military to patrol the nearby Soviet borders.

At the same time, increasing numbers of Turkish troops were sent in to ensure that martial law was enforced and the rebellions were effectively prevented. This brutal policing of its own people became a routine assignment for the Turkish army. It is amazing to realize that the majority of Turkish military activities in the last 50 years, with few exceptions, have not been against aggressive invaders or foreign armies, but rather against the Kurds.

The military presences, the threats, the forced relocations were sufficient. Atatürk's goal of one Turkey and one people had been achieved. The Kurdish movement was effectively silenced for the next 30 years.

YEARS OF SILENCE

The man who transformed Turkey died in 1938. His policies began to come into question as their resemblance to certain principles of fascism became clearer in the post-World War II period. The United States was becoming a more powerful presence in the region. And Turkey began to feel the pressure to move toward a more democratic system of government.

The biggest obstacles to Turkey's achieving a more democratic system of government lay in Islamic influences and the activities of the military. Concerns about possible Kurdish rebellions were a distant third—a worry, but one that lay behind the fears of a new and more powerful class

Mustafa Kemal Atatürk, 1932

Ataturk was a leader in the drive for Turkish liberation, who ended the Ottoman dynasty in 1923. He created the Republic of Turkey and served as its president until his death in 1938.

of Islamic clerics who were attempting to change Atatürk's plans for a secular government. The military began to interfere more actively in Turkey's government, responding to ineffective conservative administrations. The military would take over the government on several occasions, their efforts explained as the only possible way to restore order.

Military governments would, in general, mean stricter control of the Kurdish population, which was viewed as a continuing threat to Turkey's stability.

By the 1960s, the power of the Republican Party (the party of Atatürk) had faded. Many new political parties were springing up, campaigning vigorously throughout Turkey—including the Kurdish regions. As the Democratic Party won power and restored a religious presence to the state, mosques and places of worship once more began to issue the call for a return to the traditional Islamic values that had flourished under the Ottomans. Politics was awakening the Kurdish people, and their homeland became an important campaign site for the many different parties that swept through Turkey. The region was poor; increased mechanization and changes in farming had left many without jobs. They were undereducated, and living closely together. More significantly, while the rest of Turkey's population was holding fairly steady, the population in Kurdistan was nearly doubling.

A successful Kurdish rebellion in Iraq in 1961 by the Kurdistan Democratic Party (KDP) inspired the creation of a Turkish branch, known as the Kurdistan Democratic Party (KDPT). But it was a party formed and maintained in secret. Despite the explosion of political parties in the 1960s, despite a new liberalization of certain policies, including the right to freedom of the press and assembly, it remained illegal to speak the Kurdish language, or to organize a Kurdish political party.

As the 1960s drew to a close, these early efforts to organize Kurds into a more coherent political group were quickly suppressed. An increasingly large number of military groups were sent into the region to patrol the territory. Kurdish students organized a demonstration on August 3, 1967. Thousands of Kurds turned out to protest the increasingly strict military control, as well as the economic problems and the overwhelming poverty their people were suffering.

The sight of thousands of Kurds gathering was sufficient to alarm the Turkish government. Increasing numbers of troops were sent in, and thousands were arrested. The rebellion had been put down.

But a new revolution was quietly happening within Kurdish society. The political movement, the aim of nationalism, had once been almost exclusively dependent on the efforts of middle- and upper-class Kurdish leaders. But they had proved themselves inadequate to advance the cause, and increasingly content to maintain the status quo in a system that was benefiting them both economically and socially. They had lost touch with the poverty crippling much of Kurdistan.

But a new, more socialist movement was sweeping through the universities where young Kurds gathered. One university student, a young man named Abdullah Ocalan, determined to change the lives of the Kurdish people in Turkey. He would form a political party, the Workers' Party of Kurdistan (PKK), which would reinvent and redefine the Kurdish struggle.

YEARS OF STRUGGLE

In 1971, the Turkish military seized power in a coup. It would mark the beginning of yet another phase of the oppression of the Kurds. They were effectively treated as foreigners in their own land, marginalized and shut out of power unless they agreed to relinquish any connection with the customs and traditions of their past.

The majority of the rural Kurdish population still spoke Kurdish, but the law that made the use of their language illegal served to further push them to the fringes of society. Earning a living became increasingly difficult, as they were in many cases unable to communicate with Turks unless they relied on intermediaries to translate. Their schools, where they existed, were inferior, and classes were conducted in Turkish.

It is perhaps not surprising that gradually the Kurds determined that their only hope lay in armed resistance. Soon word of the activities of *pesh mergas*—freedom fighters— began to spread through Kurdish communities. These rumors also quickly traveled to Turkish authorities, who responded by once more declaring martial law in effect in the eastern Kurdish regions, particularly in Diyarbekir, where much of the rebel activity was being organized.

The Turkish president made it clear that these Kurdish rebellions would not be tolerated, when he said, "There is no room for liberated regions and activities aimed at language, racial, class or sectarian differences in our homeland. The government will defeat the disease and heads will be crushed."

But as the government launched on yet another effort to "crush" the Kurdish population, Abdullah Ocalan was organizing a movement to fight back against the oppression that had dominated Kurdish life for the past 20 years. Born in 1948, Abdullah had grown up in a peasant family and witnessed first-hand the brutal treatment his people suffered at the hands of the Turks, as well as the poverty and inferior conditions that marked their life. He determined to change all that. In his 20s, after being briefly jailed for political activities, he spent three years traveling throughout the Turkish regions of Kurdistan, meeting with the people and spreading a message designed to spark a revolution. The party he founded with six of his friends in 1974, the PKK, had a socialist plan for the governing of an independent Kurdistan.

A critical element of the PKK's plan was to break with the past, to no longer rely on the Kurdish leaders who had

Abdullah Ocalan, 1999

Ocalan founded the PKK (Workers' Party of Kurdistan) with six of his friends in 1974. This group had a socialist plan for governing a proposed independent Kurdistan.

traditionally governed the region and represented its interests to Turkish authorities. The roots of this system of leadership lay in the system of aghas and shaikhs, and these leaders had proved themselves unable to effectively lead the Kurds out of the poverty and brutal conditions that kept the people suppressed and oppressed.

The PKK soon made it clear that it would not accept the status quo, nor would it work within the system to effect change politically. Turkey, it argued, was using violent tactics to control the Kurdish population. The PKK intended to fight back.

THE PKK

When earlier Kurdish political representatives, drawn from the upper- and middle-class, had attempted to advance the cause of Kurdish independence, their efforts had been for the most part based on working within the system, and in creating a new political order similar to that which had existed under the Ottomans. They envisioned a Kurdistan ruled by the same religious and tribal leaders who had traditionally governed the Kurds.

The PKK represented a truly revolutionary break with the past. They had no interest in re-creating a system that had benefited a few through the efforts of many. Instead, they focused on the rights of workers, as well as Kurds. The majority of the members of the PKK were from the working class. Their philosophy was based more on Marxism than on Islam. It was not merely a civil war, but also a class war, that the PKK was intent on launching.

The PKK soon began to make their more aggressive stance clear, initiating a series of attacks on the towns of Eruh and Shemdinli in August of 1984. When the conflict had ended, 24 soldiers and nine civilians had been killed. In September, another conflict ended with the deaths of 12 Turkish soldiers.

But the PKK's attacks were not limited to military bases. In addition to ambushing troops, the PKK also began killing wealthy landowners.

Initially, the PKK's violent guerilla tactics repulsed the

average Kurd. Rather than being inspired to join the cause and fight for a free state, most Kurds were disturbed by the PKK's willingness to murder the aghas who, in the minds of many Kurds, were the traditional leaders of their community but who, to the PKK, were accomplices to the Turkish government's efforts to eliminate all traces of Kurdish opposition. Kurdish villagers frequently found themselves caught in the middle between two equally violent forces, threatened if they did not assist the PKK, and then threatened again if they did.

Because the PKK was striking locally, against individual landowners, the government decided that it could no longer rely on its troops stationed in the region. If the PKK was bringing the battles home, the government reasoned, it needed to respond in kind. As a result, the Village Law was passed in April 1985, which in essence gave the government the right to hire "temporary village guards," arming local citizens to fight against the PKK. The guards were paid well for their service, and the government had little trouble finding men to fill the post.

The PKK took many of its supplies from other Kurdish outposts in neighboring countries, particularly Iraq. By 1987, the village guards were charged not only with keeping the peace in their region, but also with policing the territory to block PKK access to supplies and weapons. The PKK fought back with force. The village guards had no telephones or radios, and were spread thin across the region, with no more than six guards in a single location. The PKK moved in on the guards, and brutally killed them and their families.

These intimidation tactics, designed to drive the Kurdistan population away from the guards, sparked a fierce government response. Attempts to further wipe out Kurdish culture included refusing to give birth certificates to children registered with Kurdish names. The government drastically increased the number of soldiers sent to patrol Kurdistan. In the 1980s, roughly two-thirds of the Turkish army was in the Kurdish regions, patrolling their own people. By 1987, a state of emergency was declared in eight Kurdish provinces and a governor-general was appointed to coordinate the efforts of the various forces fighting the PKK. The governor-general was given wide-ranging powers, including the ability to evacuate villages if he felt it was necessary. Torture and physical abuse were common, and hundreds of villagers were routinely arrested and beaten until they confessed to aiding the PKK efforts. Villages suspected of harboring PKK activists were evacuated, and the homes burned. Hundreds of thousands of Kurds were left homeless.

These efforts backfired horribly. The majority of Kurdish villagers had not initially supported the PKK's campaign of intimidation and its arbitrary murder of landlords and village guards. But the brutal and violent methods of the government eclipsed those used by the PKK, and resulted in Kurdish families living in constant fear of imprisonment and abuse at the hands of the government. The number of Kurds supporting the PKK increased steadily.

In an effort to stamp out the PKK's newfound success in recruiting more support, the President of Turkey, President Turgut Ozal, announced that any Turkish publishing house that "falsely reflected events in the region" would be closed down. This clear attempt at censorship outraged the majority of those working in the media, whether or not they supported the PKK. The same law, Kararname 413, gave the governor-general of Kurdistan the right to relocate anyone he thought needed to be moved out of the region to an area determined by the government. Hundreds of villages were burned following the passing of this law, and thousands left homeless.

The outcry amongst politicians and the Turkish people

Refugee camp in Northern Iraq

Brutal and violent methods of the Turkish military left many Kurds homeless and created a refugee crisis throughout the region.

to these brutal actions now joined the protests of the Kurdish population. The images of their own country-men turned into refugees by the Turkish military was repugnant to the average person, and the government soon realized that the crisis had gone from a regional to a national one.

At nearly the same time, south of Turkey in Iraq,

Saddam Hussein was brutally murdering the Kurdish population within Iraqi territory. Nearly 60,000 refugees from Iraq flooded the Turkish borders, seeking asylum within Kurdistan.

THE 1990S AND BEYOND

The refugee crisis forced the Turkish government to rethink its approach to the Kurdish crisis. By 1992, President Ozal had determined that a political solution might be preferable to the ongoing cycle of violence. He suggested that the PKK might possibly become a participant in Turkey's political system. The PKK responded with a brief ceasefire in March of 1993, but the overtures for peaceful compromise made by President Ozal vanished when he died on April 17, 1993. The new President, Sulayman Demirel, was less willing to negotiate with the PKK, and allowed the army to capitalize on the ceasefire by rounding up as many PKK fighters as it could find. For six weeks, the army killed about 100 people (fighters and civilians), arrested hundreds more, and resumed their destruction of homes and whole villages. The chance for peace had vanished.

Following the path tread by so many other guerrilla groups, the PKK determined to make it clear that theirs was not a local problem, one that could be settled by sending more and more troops into the Kurdish region. They decided to take their fight to the rest of Turkey. Tourist sites in southern Turkey were attacked. European tourists in Kurdistan were seized as hostages. Turkish embassies and business locations in Europe were targeted and attacked.

The government responded brutally and with force. Armed Turkish forces would enter a village suspected of harboring PKK activists and randomly seize and arrest (and often torture) villagers. The more violent the government's oppression, the more Kurds flocked to the PKK. Where just a short time before large numbers of Kurdish refugees had crossed over into Turkey from Iraq, now the tide turned the other way, as safety was thought to be more assured on the other side of the border.

The national nightmare was rapidly becoming a foreign policy disaster. As Turkey sought to establish itself as an active and democratic participant in the international community, these human rights abuses against its own people made investors and diplomats wary. The brutality of the military raised questions about the true nature of the Turkish government. And as more Kurds were heard calling for autonomy, or the right to govern their own region, rather than complete independence and separation from Turkey, the horrific response of the Turkish government was increasingly difficult to understand or excuse.

Group of Iraqi Kurds, c. 1914

Photographs of Iraqi Kurds are rare. This photograph was taken by Captain T.A. O'Connor, a cartographer. O'Connor assisted in mapping the route for the Baghdad to Samarra' railroad, which was completed just prior to World War I.

Baghdad is the capital of Iraq and Samarra' is located in the central part of that country. Prior to 1918, the Ottoman Empire controlled the area.

4

The Kurds
in Iraq

n April 15, 1987, the war between Iran and Iraq that had polarized much of the Middle East entered a new phase. On that date, a formation of Iraqi war planes targeted 13 towns and villages, dropping lethal loads of mustard gas on the helpless population below. By the end of the month, some 30 towns had been similarly targeted, and by the middle of the year, Iraqi planes were dropping chemical weapons on their targets on a daily basis.

These chemical weapons produced horrifying numbers of casualties during their use from 1987 to 1988. But the casualties were not Iranians. The population that Saddam Hussein had targeted, the citizens upon whom his chemical weapons were dropping, were his own people. Or, more specifically, they were Kurds.

Young Kurdish Refugee Girl, 1991

By March 1991, more that one and a half million Kurds were fleeing across the snowy mountains of Kurdistan, heading for refuge in Turkey, Iran, Syria, or anywhere else to get away from extermination through Saddam Hussein's rain of chemical weapons on the civilian Kurdish populations.

By March of 1991, more than one-and-a half million Kurds would be fleeing across the snowy mountains of Kurdistan, heading for refuge in Turkey, in Iran or in Syria. Their stories—of thousands of villages being destroyed, of the horror of mustard gas and nerve gas raining down on them from their own armed forces—of hundreds of thousands of Kurdish men, women and children being exterminated—finally brought the Kurdish crisis to international prominence.

It is important to understand the history of the Kurds in Iraq to better appreciate the tragic sequence of events that led to this horrifying example of genocide.

TREATIES MADE AND BROKEN

The Kurdish territories of Iraq lie, for the most part, along its northeastern corners. Portions of this region are rich and fertile, stretching across a mountainous area and including fertile plains crossed by four rivers. The Hamrin Mountains act as a barrier, separating the Kurdish provinces from other parts of Iraq.

The area produces many of the same crops as other Kurdish territories—tobacco, wood, wool, dairy products—but its greatest source of riches lie in the oil deposits that have made the region so valuable, particularly those found in the city of Kirkuk. The Kurds (who make up approximately 17 percent of the population of Iraq) receive little benefit from the oil; instead it has proved simply one more obstacle to their independence.

The nation we know today as Iraq was once part of the vast Ottoman Empire. In the aftermath of World War I, as parts of the Middle East were being carved up by the victorious Allied powers, the rich oil fields of the province of Mosul made the region a particularly attractive prize. Britain proved the winner of this prize, conquering the region from the retreating Ottomans over a four-year period from 1914 to 1918.

The oil-rich territory, once won, would become the subject of intense debate among experts in the region about how best to govern this new piece of the British Empire. Some felt that it should become a British protectorate, linked to India and governed by Indian immigrants as a kind of reward for their brave service during World War I. Others felt strongly that Britain's interests would be best safeguarded by having the new territory governed by Arabs, and their opinion ultimately won the debate.

Within the framework of this new Arab country, tentative plans were made to create a Kurdish state in the region where Kurds formed more than one-half of the population. This Kurdish state would be semi-autonomous, linked to the Arab state but providing a limited opportunity for the Kurds to govern themselves under British administration.

It was an opportunity that the Kurds would not be able to seize. As in Turkey, they proved their own worst enemy at this critical early stage following the fall of the Ottoman Empire. The population proved disorganized and divided, with Kurds in the northern part of the new region claiming closer ties to Kurds in Turkey. Cultural and ethnic divisions prevented any kind of unity between nomadic Kurds and those living in more urban areas. Some clans were willing to follow the guidelines only of their own shaikhs, and refused to respond to any other authority. Disputes amongst the shaikhs made cooperation with British authorities nearly impossible.

British officials proposed first one possible leader than another, but representatives from one tribe refused to be governed by a shaikh from another. Some Kurds pushed British officials and representatives of the League of

Kurds, Turkish-Iraqi Border, 1919

This photograph was taken by Major Kenneth Mason. When World War I ended in November 1918, Major Mason was ordered to obtain preliminary agreements of friendship between the Kurds and Great Britain.

He noted in his report that: "Every one in the Kurdistan carries a rifle from the age of about eight upwards, and all are swathed in two or three enormous belts or bandoliers of cartridges. They look like stage brigands [robbers] I suppose naturally, since brigandage [robbery] is their normal calling. I do not see how we are to stop them from carrying arms."

Nations for a separate Kurd state that would include the Kurds in Turkey; while others claimed that they wanted to be part of the greater country of Iraq.

There were economic difficulties as well. The Kurdistan region of Iraq was dependent for supplies and trade on Arab communities. There was no independent infrastructure that could have supported a separate economy, nor did the

Kurds take any kind of clear-cut steps at this critical period to create one.

The victory of Mustafa Kemal and his supporters in Turkey forced the Allies to consider many of the elements of the Treaty of Sèvres null and void, as this treaty had been negotiated with an entity (the Ottoman Empire) that no longer existed. Representatives from the Allied powers gathered in Lausanne, Switzerland to examine the various points of contention with the old treaty. Despite the fact that it would soon decide their respective fates, there were no representatives from either the Kurdish or the Arab sides at the conference.

And yet the Kurds were discussed in great detail. The territory of Mosul—a territory deemed Kurdish by the Sèvres treaty—was full of oil and thus highly desirable to both the British and Turks. Both sides used the plight of the Kurds, and their own willingness to put the Kurds' interest first, as central to their argument for why Mosul should be granted to them.

The truth was, of course, quite different. Mosul lay directly along the frontier between the new territories. A granting of Mosul to one side (the newly formed Republic of Turkey) or the other (the Arab kingdom of Iraq, represented by British administrators) would have strategic and political implications as the borders were re-drawn.

The Treaty of Lausanne was signed on July 24, 1923, overruling any earlier decisions declared as part of the Treaty of Sèvres.

THE BRITISH PROMISE

By the time that Britain prepared to grant Iraq its independence, Iraqi officials had reassured the British that they would not follow the example of Turkey. There was no need to take additional steps to provide a separate region for

Kurdish Tents, c. 1902

Ellsworth Huntington, the American geographer, photographed these Kurdish tents in the mountain region northwest of Mosul.

the Kurds, they claimed. Within Iraq, the Kurds would be allowed to speak their own language (or languages), attend Kurdish schools, and govern their own territory.

But the Kurds were not satisfied with these promises, particularly since they did not exist in written form in any of the treaties that were being drafted to formalize Iraq's independence. In the town of Sulaymaniya, elections scheduled to be held in September of 1930 quickly resulted in mass demonstrations and strikes by Kurds who felt that the new government would not represent their interests. Army and police had been called in to keep the peace; their presence did exactly the opposite. An attempt to boycott the elections as a protest against policies deemed unfair to Kurds quickly transformed into a riot, and many Kurds, including the popular Shaikh Madmud Barzinji, were arrested.

As the date of Iraq's independence drew near, the League of Nations made clear that it was the responsibility of Britain to assure that the rights of the Kurds were not trampled on or erased in the process. It was a responsibility that Britain largely failed to fulfill. The promises the British had made when they first arrived in the region proved false.

Following the initial round of protests, as the new kingdom of Iraq began to assert its authority over the Kurds the situation quieted. The king of Iraq, King Faysal, allowed the aghas and shaikhs to retain a certain amount of control over their tribes, and provided that they assured that taxes were paid promptly and the peace was maintained, a kind of passive coexistence marked the climate of the region.

This would change with the death of the Iraqi king in 1933. The king had been a moderating and unifying force, but in his absence, different factions began to compete for power. The Kurds were quick to join this competition for new rights in the absence of an authoritative central government. In 1935, a group of some 40 Kurdish chiefs came together and launched an official protest that the promises made by the League of Nations in 1926— including that Kurdish would be declared the official language in their region—had not been kept. In addition, they requested the right to elect their own representatives to the national legislature—seeking not the right to completely govern themselves, but the right to elect Kurdish representatives to help determine Iraqi national policy. Their demands were generally ignored.

With so many competing forces attempting to seize

control of the national government, politicians had little time for the demands of a handful of Kurdish chiefs. It was thought that they were looking out for their own interests; that by and large they did not speak for the majority of Kurds living in Iraq.

In a sense, this was correct. A movement was growing among Kurds, as a new group of younger, educated Kurds began to advance the cause of Kurdish nationalism. They had become disaffected by the attitudes and actions of the aghas and shaikhs, who acted most often out of self-interest rather than in an effort to advance the cause of the Kurdish people. Those who had benefited from the system, who had grown wealthy and operated through connections with the king and other well-placed officials, were unlikely to spark a revolutionary movement to radically transform the life of the average Kurd. But this new group of activists, whose goals were closer to socialism than tribalism, had dreams of creating a homeland for their people.

This new group of young Kurds gathered together in Baghdad, the capital of Iraq. They had come to be educated in the center of this new nation, but their schooling would provide them with the opportunity to see, close-up, the inner workings of the government. These students formed a few small cultural clubs, whose goals were to foster discussion of Kurdish language and literature, but soon the conversations turned to focus on Kurdish heritage and then to Kurdish rights.

This growing sense of ethnic heritage among educated young Kurds coincided with the rise of a new movement sweeping through Iraq and other parts of the Middle East. This new movement spoke of the common heritage and goals of Arabs, suggesting that their focus should be on a single Arabic movement, rather than separatist and often-conflicting national goals. Supporters of this view, the Pan-Arabists, regarded with suspicion and hostility those attempting to advance smaller, ethnically based causes, like the Kurds, and conflict was inevitable. The backlash against the Kurds within Iraq actually served to strengthen their cause, prompting more Kurds to rally around their own movement under increasingly hostile words and actions from Pan-Arabists within Iraq.

A number of Kurdish groups began to spring up, some with links to the Iraqi Communist Party, others tied to a particular class (wealthy urban young men, religious figures, etc.). One radical group, known as *Darkar* (Woodcutters), spun off its own political party, called *Hiwa* (Hope). This party had a radical goal—to unify many of the different, smaller Kurdish groups that had been springing up under a single banner, one of nationalism and freedom for Kurds. Hiwa soon had several chapters in the major cities and university campuses of Iraq, a sign that the stereotypical impression of Kurds as rural, uneducated residents of the mountainous regions was not a reflection of where Kurdish nationalism was growing.

In fact, the movement suffered in a sense for this very transformation. Rather than attempting to woo residents of the traditional Kurdish strongholds in the mountains, Hiwa's members remained almost exclusively urban. No attempt was made to mobilize the rural Kurds to the cause, and for this reason, Hiwa remained unable to mount a serious threat to the Iraqi government.

MULLA MUSTAFA BARZANI

The rebellion launched by Mulla Mustafa Barzani offers an interesting example of the weaknesses that prevented the Kurds from coming together in a unified fashion to advance their own cause. Mulla Mustafa Barzani was an agha, a member of the great Barzani tribe that had maintained control for several generations over the rough and wild territory in northeastern Iraq. When the Iraqi government attempted to resettle Assyrian Christians in his area, and to add police to monitor them and taxes to support the government, Mulla Mustafa decided to fight back. After a series of bitter battles, Mulla Mustafa, his older brother and several members of his family fled across the border to Turkey, where they were captured.

By 1943, Mulla Mustafa was back in his home territory, surrounded by an increasingly large group of supporters. His initial request to the Iraqi government was simple and straightforward: he wanted the government to grant him and his brother the right to live peacefully in the same region where their family had lived for several generations. The response? A police force was sent to arrest Mulla Mustafa—viewed as a fugitive by the government. Fighting broke out, and a request for amnesty was transformed into an armed battle by an incompetent series of actions by the Iraqi administration.

At this stage, Iraqi officials made the mistake of continuing to engage Mulla Mustafa and his forces, and he was soon transformed into a kind of folk hero, a symbol of Kurdish nationalism, as he and his men fought off attempts by armed forces to keep them under control. After four months of skirmishes, the Iraqi government reluctantly offered Mulla Mustafa a pardon, but by now he had no interest in accepting their offer.

Mulla Mustafa had received offers of support from many different tribes, and he also began to look for help from a new source—the British. Mulla Mustafa understood that the British were dissatisfied with the general direction of the new Iraqi government, and displeased with the decreasing amount of influence they were able to wield over a region that had been intended to serve as a base for British interests in the Middle East. Mulla Mustafa began to correspond with British officials, offering them the opportunity to support a

Iraqi Tribesmen with a Royal Air Force Officer, 1944

The British attempted to control the direction of the new Iraqi government and one of the ways it did this was to train Iraqis in military maneuvers. These tribesmen, including Kurds, Assyrians, Arabs, and Baluchs were trained as paratroopers and taught all forms of warfare from unarmed combat to the use of the latest weapons.

Kurdish state (one under his leadership) in exchange for a firmer ally in the region. But the British refused.

Mulla Mustafa also received visits from several members of Hiwa, who were anxious to steer the rebellion in a direction that would serve their party's aims. But Mulla Mustafa was unwilling, wisely understanding that the ultimate goals of Hiwa would greatly conflict with his own.

Several attempts by the Iraqi government to broker an agreement were refused by Mulla Mustafa, who felt that he had the upper hand, and he began to issue demands for the release of Kurdish political prisoners, for a Kurdish commissioner to be appointed who would have the right to veto any national decision deemed detrimental to Kurdish interests, and for a personal gift of more than $200,000 under the category of "agricultural loan." Obviously a great deal had changed since Mulla Mustafa's initial request for the freedom to live in his native village, and Iraqi officials had had enough. In August of 1945, the army moved in, soon joined by Kurdish tribes unwilling to allow Mulla Mustafa to become their leader. Within two months, Mulla Mustafa's forces had been defeated and their leader was forced to flee to Mahabad, in western Iran. But Iraq had not heard the last of Mulla Mustafa.

THE EFFECTS OF THE BARZANI REBELLION

The rapidity with which Mulla Mustafa had been able to gather an armed force of supporters, his successful challenge to the Iraqi leadership, proved that the Kurdish nationalist movement still existed, that there was an ethnic sentiment and a sense of discontent brewing in both the mountains and the university towns, waiting to be harnessed.

The rebellion caused a split in Hiwa, dividing those who believed that a nationalist movement could best be sparked by the actions of traditional leaders—shaikhs and aghas like Mulla Mustafa—and those who wanted a complete break with the old order and the old way of thinking. It was in the latter group, those loosely affiliated with the Iraqi Communists, that a new party would spring up that would shape the next stage of the Kurdish movement. In 1945, *Rizgari Kurd* (Kurdish Liberation) was formed; its goal was to set free and then unify all of Kurdistan. As initial steps toward this goal, Rizgari Kurd determined to achieve some sort of self-government within Iraq and to build links with non-Iraqi Kurdish parties.

In January of 1946, the United Nations received an appeal from Rizgari Kurd to resolve the situation of the Kurds by granting them the right to govern themselves within their own nation. By now, the Iraqi officials were no longer willing to dismiss the movement as the actions of a few students. Many of the members of Rizgari Kurd were arrested.

Rizgari Kurd eventually disappeared, but not because of threats from the Iraqi government. Instead, the end of the party came about because of actions from the revolutionary in exile, Mulla Mustafa.

Operating from Iran, Mulla Mustafa had taken steps to create a new party, the Iraqi Kurdish Democratic Party (KDP). As a national hero, Mulla Mustafa had the credentials to gather a wide range of Kurds around him, and his plans to unify all Iraqi Kurds under a single party drew an immediate response. Rizgari Kurd members were divided over the formation of the KDP. Some felt that Mulla Mustafa's popularity and status might be the only way to gather all Kurds together to fight for independence. Others felt that his plans to mobilize an Iraqi Kurdish party conflicted with Rizgari Kurd's goals to achieve a homeland for all Kurds, not merely those living within Iraqi borders. The conflict would bring the end of Rizgari Kurd.

The Kurdish Democratic Party soon changed its name to the Kurdistan Democratic Party, demonstrating that it was fighting for the rights of anyone living within Kurdistan, not simply the Kurds. Gradually, it became more leftist in its policy plans, focusing more on agricultural reform and workers' rights. But it still remained closely tied to the aghas and shaikhs, relying on them for support and so, unwilling to risk policies that might offend these tribal chiefs.

Gradually, various Kurdish factions joined together under the single banner of the KDP. The climate within Iraq was changing. The Pan-Arab movement was growing, particularly under the encouragement of the dynamic President Nasser governing Egypt. Other factions were rising up within Iraq as well—socialists, liberals, right-wing Islamic groups. The days of the Iraqi monarchy were numbered. The Kurds wanted to ensure that their interests would be respected by whatever form of government came next.

REVOLUTION IN IRAQ

On July 14, 1958, a group of military officers overthrew the Iraqi monarchy and set up a new government, declaring that Iraq would become a democratic republic. It was a hopeful sign for the Kurds that a Kurd was included in the three-member "Sovereignty Council" established by Iraq's new leader, General Qasim. The KDP immediately declared its support for the new government, looking forward to new opportunities for Kurds to work within the system.

These hopes were short-lived. As with any leader who seizes power suddenly and violently, Qasim's focus soon turned to eliminating any challengers, to ensure that no one rose up to test his authority. He had no intention of granting too much power to any group, including the Kurds, nor did he want to alienate any other group of Iraqis at this critical early stage.

Qasim decided to make a concession to the Kurds, in the hopes of buying more time. He invited Mulla Mustafa to Baghdad, ending his exile and giving him the right to become chairman of the KDP. Mulla Mustafa received a hero's welcome upon his return, and he was set up, thanks to Qasim, in Baghdad with his own impressive home, an official car and a monthly salary.

Mulla Mustafa soon earned his money. In March of 1959, a group opposed to Qasim's leadership, including Pan-Arabs and supporters of the Iraqi monarchy, launched a revolt in Mosul. Mulla Mustafa gathered together a force of Kurdish fighters and Communists and the revolt was quickly and brutally stamped out.

The next challenge came to Qasim from the Communists, who launched a rebellion in the city of Kirkuk, where unemployment was high and dissatisfaction with the revolutionary government was higher. The Communists had determined that their political support entitled them to a more prominent position within the government. Qasim ordered Mulla Mustafa to make sure that this threat was eliminated, and he quickly complied. In return, Qasim legalized the KDP and awarded Mulla Mustafa a stretch of Barzani land that had been seized by the previous Iraqi government.

Mulla Mustafa, strengthened by his position as a close ally of Qasim, determined to cement his own power base. He launched a series of attacks against Kurdish leaders who had not supported him, including many of those who had helped the Iraqi army force him into exile many years ago. As one by one these old enemies were assassinated or forced to flee, Qasim suddenly realized that his Kurdish ally was becoming increasingly powerful and ruthless.

It did not take long for Qasim to begin to build alliances with some of Mulla Mustafa's enemies, giving them arms and increasingly voicing public support for them at Mulla Mustafa's expense. By the fall of 1960, it was clear that Mulla Mustafa was no longer viewed as a friend to the government. His brother was charged with creating "national dissension"; he quickly went into hiding. By the end of the year, Mulla Mustafa had lost his house, car and salary, and Qasim would no longer meet with him. The alliance between the revolutionary government and the Kurds had ended.

THE KURDISH WAR

By the winter that spread from 1960 to 1961, Kurdish dissatisfaction with the Qasim government had expanded. The government had instituted a series of land and tobacco taxes that hit particularly hard in the Kurdish regions, and many of the aghas were disturbed at recent efforts to legislate agricultural land reforms that would affect much of the feudal landholdings.

Mulla Mustafa saw a chance to take his feud with Qasim to the next level. Following a series of negotiations with other tribal chiefs and local Kurds, he began a revolt against the government. The revolt soon turned to war, with fierce clashes between armed Kurds and the Iraqi military. Supported by neighboring Iran and Turkey, who were willing to assist the Kurdish rebels provided that they kept their nationalism within Iraqi borders, the conflict lasted through the overthrow of the Qasim government and two more short-lived administrations before a ceasefire was negotiated in February 1964.

The ceasefire caused yet another split within the Kurdish ranks, as members of the KDP expressed their dismay at Mulla Mustafa's willingness to negotiate without consulting the rest of the party. It was a split that would not heal. The KDP felt that its goals of self-rule for the Kurdish people would never be brought about by an agha like Mulla Mustafa. Mulla Mustafa would go on to negotiate with the national government to institute reforms that would help alleviate some of the suffering in Kurdish regions. But the conflicts within Kurdish ranks, as well as between Kurds and the Iraqi government, were not fully resolved when a new party, the Ba'th party, overthrew the government and seized power.

Kurdish Rebels Standing in the Ruins of a Village near Chami Razan, Iraq

The Kurdish rebels continued to demand an independent state for the 2 million Kurds in northern Iraq. This revolt was supported by neighboring Iran and Turkey, but most political observers felt that any nation of Kurdistan would necessarily embrace the 8 million Kurds in Turkey and Iran, as well.

The Ba'ths were no friends of Mulla Mustafa. Many of their members had been killed by his forces when he and Qasim cooperated to eliminate many of Qasim's enemies in 1959. Fighting between Mulla Mustafa's forces and the Iraqi military started up in June 1963. It lasted for about five months, before the Ba'th government was overthrown.

It is worth noting that the Ba'th regime, which returned to power again in 1968, had initially directed its hostility toward Mulla Mustafa personally, not towards the Kurds in a more general sense. Early on, the Ba'ths had stated that the resolution of the Kurdish question and an effort to maintain peace with the Kurds would be critical elements of their political platform. Their quarrel was not with the Kurds; it was only with Mulla Mustafa.

Inevitably, yet another split resulted when the Ba'th regime extended an offer of equal national rights for Kurds. Supporters of Mulla Mustafa rejected it, while others within the KDP wanted to take advantage of this opportunity for peace and progress. Finally, a peace agreement was announced on March 11, 1970, following 10 years of bloody battles. Thousands of deaths, thousands of destroyed homes, hundreds of thousands made home-less bore witness to the cost of this civil war. But the agreement made it seem as if the Kurds had at last won. It granted them participation in government, including appointments to senior national positions; it stated that schools in Kurdish regions would teach both Arabic and Kurdish; it required that officials in Kurdish areas speak Kurdish; it granted the Kurds the right to set up their own organizations; it promised economic develop-ment of Kurdish regions; and it declared the formation of a Kurdish area that would be self-governing.

The hopes that sprang up after this agreement was signed would be short-lived. Neither side fully trusted the other—and with good reason. Mulla Mustafa continued to receive weapons from Iran, and built ties with the U.S. and Israel that increased his supplies and control over the Kurdish region. Disputes sprang up over precisely which regions would be deemed "Kurdish majority"—the government was unwilling to place oil-rich areas like Kirkuk outside of the national control. Mulla

Mustafa claimed that the Iraqi administration was juggling the numbers by bringing large numbers of Arabs into Kurdish regions to avoid them falling into the "Kurdish majority" category.

Two attempts on Mulla Mustafa's life (in 1971 and 1972) made it clear that the peace agreement was falling apart. It seemed obvious that the Ba'th would proceed with its own plans for governing Iraq, with or without Kurdish cooperation.

While Mulla Mustafa is regarded as a hero by many Kurds, a symbol of the struggle against Iraqi domination, many of his actions were designed to advance his own interests and did little to assist the Kurds to create their own state. His negotiations with Iranian, American, and Israeli representatives enriched him personally and increased his power, but did little to advance the cause of Kurdish self-government. The Iraqi government could not permit someone to obtain weapons and assistance from foreign governments, nor could it allow its authority in critical oil regions to be challenged.

War broke out in 1974, and the Kurdish forces were quickly pushed back. Iran soon moved in to arm the Kurds. Fighting continued into 1975, intensifying to the point where the only clear next step was out-and-out war between Iraq and Iran, an option neither side wanted. A meeting was called between the Shah of Iran and the Iraqi Vice-President. At its conclusion, an agreement had been reached. Iraq willingly gave up a disputed waterway. Iran agreed to seal its borders, preventing Kurds from traveling into or out of Iran. The Iraqi Vice-President, Saddam Hussein, had successfully brought an end to the Kurdish war. Mulla Mustafa fled the country. He died in the United States in March 1979, following a battle with cancer. The Kurds would be left to struggle on without him.

Iran-Iraq War, 1980-85

The Iran-Iraq war lasted from 1980 to 1985. These are Iraqi soldiers on a pontoon bridge at Khorramshahr in southern Iraq. This area was the scene of heavy fighting during the war.

IRAN-IRAQ WAR

The recent history of the Kurdish people is sprinkled with opportunities lost, moments when a more unified and cohesive group might have been able to negotiate from a position of strength. During the Iran-Iraq War, which lasted from 1980 to 1985, the Kurds had yet another chance to achieve at least some of their goals. But the gap between Kurds on either side of the border had widened, and they were unable to agree on their goals or the steps they would need to take to achieve them. Once more, internal disunity prevented the Kurds from moving forward.

The Kurds had continued to wage an internal war with the Iraqi government, now headed by Saddam Hussein as its president. A new party, the Patriotic Union of Kurdistan (PUK), was engaged in an ongoing armed conflict with Iraqi forces, engaging them at a point when they were desperately needed to fight off the Iranian army. A brief cease-fire was negotiated in December 1983, although each side agreed to its limited terms more to buy time than in the hopes of achieving any long-term goals. The agreement did not last long, and by 1987 the PUK had formed a coalition with other Kurdish groups in an effort to spark the over-throw of Saddam Hussein's government. Their goals were clear: an end to the Iran-Iraq war and the right to govern themselves. They joined with Iranian forces in battling the Iraqi military in the mountainous regions of the north.

It is not surprising that the Iraqi government viewed this as treason. The response was swift and brutal. Thousands of Kurdish citizens were forcibly removed from their homes. Large chunks of Kurdish territory were declared "free fire zones"—anyone found there could be shot. The military moved into Kurdish territory, extending from Zakho in the north to Halabja in the south and Sulaymaniya in the east, destroying thousands of towns and removing nearly 300,000 Kurds to "detention camps" in southern and western Iraq. Then came the chemical weapons.

Beginning on April 15, 1987, planes began dropping chemical weapons on Kurdish villages, as well as camps where Kurdish rebels were suspected of hiding. Mustard gas was used first. Then the campaign entered a new and more horrible phase.

Between February and October of 1988, Saddam Hussein's forces carried out a special operation, code-named *Anfal* (an Arabic word meaning "spoils of battle"). In the Koran, Anfal is the title of a chapter detailing the rules of war and conquest. For the Iraqi military, Anfal signaled a campaign to destroy the Kurds.

During the months of 1988 when the Ba'th forces attempted to exterminate the Kurdish population, reports of horrors trickled out. But perhaps the most brutal attack took place on March 16, when the village of Halabja lost some 5,000 people following a chemical weapon attack by their own government. In subsequent months, air campaigns targeted the Kurdish regions near the Turkish border. Thousands of innocent Kurds were killed, thousands more were captured, tortured and killed in concentration camps.

The pleas of the Kurds—to the United Nations, to other world leaders—were largely ignored. The promises the Kurdish forces had received, particularly for American assistance, were empty. The U.S. was more interested in taking advantage of the Iran/Iraq conflict to thwart the influence of the Soviet Union in the region. In the 1970s and the 1980s, the Kurds failed to fully understand that Iran/Iraq wars could end without the overthrow of the Iraqi government, leaving them paying the price for the conflict. It was a lesson bitterly learned only at the cost of thousands of Kurdish lives.

Persian Kurds, 1912

Before the automobile, an animal provided transportation for both people and for conveying goods.

5

The Kurds
in Iran

he Kurds in Iran are concentrated in an area of about
50,000 square miles in a wooded, mountainous terrain
that stretches from Mount Ararat in the north to the
Zagros Mountains. As in so many other parts of the Middle East that
might have formed Kurdistan, parts of the Iranian Kurdish territory
is rich with oil.

Estimates are the Kurds currently make up approximately
seven percent of the Iranian population. This minority is
undereducated, with a significant percentage of Kurds (particularly women) illiterate. Poor medical care and an absence of
economic opportunities have further crippled the region. Few
Kurdish homes have running water or electricity. In a country

that has turned back the clock in terms of its reliance on Islamic codes and regulations, the Kurdish provinces remain extraordinarily hampered by difficult living and working conditions.

The modern history of the Kurds in Iran can find its roots in the ill-fated Treaty of Sèvres. As the Ottoman Empire collapsed, Kurds in northern Iran began a revolt, encouraged by the example of the Kurds in Turkey. From 1920 to 1925, one Kurdish agha—Ismail Agha of the Shikak tribe, also known as Simko—organized a fighting force that seized the Kurdish territory west of Lake Urmiah and proclaimed an independent Kurdistan. His attempt to negotiate a coordinated effort with shaikhs in Turkey failed, and the British further muddied the waters by assisting in the rise to power of Reza Shah (the Iranian monarch) in 1925 following a coup. Five years later, Simko was invited to a meeting to negotiate a peace with the Iranian military. He agreed to attend, but upon his arrival, he was assassinated.

During World War II, the Allied forces of Britain, the U.S. and the Soviet Union entered Iran to establish a more reliable presence in the Middle East. They overthrew the dictatorship of Reza Shah and replaced it with a weaker administration under his son, Muhammad Reza Shah Pahlavi. Iran was divided into territories, with the south of the country occupied and controlled by British and American forces, and the north occupied by the Soviet military. The Mahabad region, in western Iran, was not occupied by any foreign forces, and a strong Kurdish movement soon sprang up in the area, supported by well-educated, middle-class, urban citizens. By 1945, a political party, the Kurdish Democratic Party, had been formed and had issued its political program, requesting self-government and autonomy for the Kurds in Iran; the opportunity to study Kurdish and to use it in the region's

administration; and the right to elect their own representatives to state and local office.

In the absence of a strong national government, this
Kurdish independence movement flourished. On January
24, 1946, the first Soviet-supported Kurdish republic was
declared—a republic that would last less than a year, but
that during that time would achieve a number of its goals,
including greater Kurdish representation in the region and
increased economic prosperity. The new republic of
Mahabad even had its own flag—a red, white, and green
banner containing a sun surrounded by wheat with a quill
in the middle. The sun signified freedom, while the quill
emphasized the importance of education.

It is interesting that there were conflicting ideas about
exactly what this new state was—was it an independent
republic, or a self-governing region within Iran? The two
different names used for the new entity—the National
Government of Kurdistan (*Houkoumati Milli Kurdistan*)
and State of the Kurdish Republic (*Dawlati Djumhouri
Kurdistan*)—underscored the confusion and demon-
strated that the new government needed to more clearly
define itself before it could make any kind of significant
political progress.

Within six months after the end of World War II,
the occupying Allied armies began to pull out of Iran.
The days of the Kurdish republic were numbered from
the moment that the troops began to leave. By the fall of
1946, the Iranian government had called for new
elections to restructure the government. To help "supervise"
the election process, Iranian troops were sent into the
Kurdish region. As the troops arrived, many Kurdish
leaders fled for friendlier borders. Others remained and
were arrested. Qazi Mohammed, who had been elected
President of the Kurdish Republic, was hanged in the
public square of Mahabad. In many other Kurdish

towns, supporters of the short-lived republic were also seized and executed.

A CRUSHED MOVEMENT

For the next 20 years, the Kurdish movement failed to evoke any kind of significant change in Iran. Many of the leaders who had helped found the Kurdish Republic were dead or in prison. But their spirit had not been erased from the region. In elections held in Mahabad in 1952, six years after the Republic had been crushed, a KDP candidate stood for election and received more than 80 percent of the vote. The elections were immediately declared improper, and a religious cleric from the Iranian capital, Tehran, was appointed the region's representative instead.

On August 19, 1953, the U.S. Central Intelligence Agency (CIA) organized a coup to install a government in Iran that would be friendlier to U.S. interests, particularly in terms of oil supply. The previous government had, with active support from the Kurdish region, nationalized the oil industry, an action that was swiftly revoked by the government put in place in 1953.

As we have seen in the last chapter, Kurdish activities in Iraq had an effect on the Kurdish movement in Iran, and vice versa. In 1958, the revolution in Iraq sparked a growth in Kurdish organizations, including organizations based in Iran. The Iranian government, sensing trouble, attempted to crack down on Kurdish activities, arresting hundreds of KDP members or suspected members.

The Shah of Iran soon attempted a new strategy—he would help the Kurds, or more specifically, help one Kurd in particular. His choice: Mulla Mustafa Barzani. The Shah determined to assist Mulla Mustafa in his efforts to overthrow the Iraqi government for strategic reasons.

Shah of Iran, Mohammad Reza Pahlavi, 1950

The Shah aided Mulla Mustafa in his efforts to overthrow the Iraqi government, but ironically he brutally cracked down on the Kurdish movement within his own country.

He would prefer to see the government in Iraq disappear. He also wanted to make this particular Kurdish group dependent on Iranian aid, so that he would better be able to dictate terms to it.

Mulla Mustafa was, as we have seen, willing to cooperate. He accepted the Shah's aid and his terms, agreeing to work toward establishing an independent

Kurdish state within Iraq (rather than the larger goals of other Kurdish rebels who had hoped to set up an independent Kurdistan that crossed over existing national borders). The Shah believed that he might score points by indicating his willingness to help the Kurdish struggle for independence, but also break the alliance between Iraqi and Iranian Kurds and thus neutralize a potentially much larger and more dangerous group of freedom fighters.

It is ironic that the Shah who so generously supplied Mulla Mustafa's forces with money and weapons brutally cracked down on the Kurdish movement within his own country. While Mulla Mustafa and his Kurdish forces enjoyed the benefits of the Shah's finances to help feed and arm them for battle against Iraq, Kurds within Iran suffered in prison or were executed. Once more, the lack of cohesion within the Kurdish community brought about even greater hardship.

RIOTS AND REVOLUTION

During the reign of the Shah, Iran experienced remarkable economic progress. But it was prosperity enjoyed only by a select few—the Shah himself, members of his immediate family, and the wealthy upper-class citizens of Iran. Enjoying the benefit of a close relationship with the U.S., the Shah was able to build a massive and powerful army equipped with American weapons. The army was particularly powerful in Kurdistan, where citizens were so closely watched that anyone traveling from one town to another had to report their plans to the mayors of both villages, who then informed the police. All disagreements with the Shah's regime were deemed illegal. There were no political parties, no opportunities for political debate, even religious and professional organizations were made illegal. The Shah's control was complete, and Kurds were viewed with intense suspicion as possible sources of rebellion against the government.

In January 1979, the government of the Shah fell, toppled by a revolutionary movement led by an Islamic cleric, Ayatollah Khomeini. The Ayatollah had called for a new, Islamic regime in Iran, based on traditional values and the teachings of the Koran. The Ayatollah demanded an end to links with the West, which he claimed were the source of corruption, and claimed that a new government would bring about a complete transformation in Iranian society to the benefit of all who had been oppressed. The Kurds were quick to join with the revolutionary movement, hoping that a change in regime would at last mean an independent and autonomous Kurdistan.

The dream would not last long. The aims and focus of the new, revolutionary government that had seized power in Tehran were based on core tenets of Islam. Its goal was the complete unity of the entire Islamic community, both within and outside Iran. There was no room for an autonomous state within this framework. The conflict went beyond simple differences in political goals to a core understanding of Islam itself.

The revolutionary government led by the Ayatollah Khomeini was a Shi'ite Muslim regime. The Kurds were, for the most part, Sunni Muslims. The disputes between these two sects of Islam date back to the time of the Ottoman Empire. The Sunnis had supported the Ottoman leaders and regarded them as the rightful spiritual guides of the people and the legitimate successors to the prophet Mohammed. The Shi'ites had disagreed with many of the Ottoman policies and did not support their claim to be the rightful spiritual and religious leaders of the people they ruled.

As the Ayatollah began to issue a series of proclamations, it became clear that the goal of the new revolutionary regime was not merely to transform life within Iran, but to export the revolution to other Arab nations. This vision of a unified Arab world, governed by the tenets of fundamentalist Islam, held little place for a tiny autonomous state governed by Kurds. The official policy made it clear that there could be no minority group within a nation based on the principle that all Muslims were brothers, waiting to be unified.

WAR AND PEACE

On April 1, 1979, Iran formally became an Islamic republic. In the months that followed, strongly anti-Western (particularly anti-American) policies were accompanied by a move to impose *sharia* (Islamic law) within Iran, governing both legal and social matters based on the teachings of the Koran. Opponents of this new government, leftist Islamic militants known as *mujahideen*, launched a series of attacks and bombing campaigns that resulted in an intense crackdown on all opponents of the administration, including Kurds.

And then came war with Iraq. As we have seen, the Kurdish communities, both in Iran and Iraq, were trapped in the cross-fire. The Kurds in Iraq sought to assist the Iranian forces, in a misguided attempt to overthrow the regime of Saddam Hussein. When Hussein used chemical weapons on the Kurdish community, hundreds of thousands of Kurdish refugees fled from Iraq to Iran.

The Kurds, throughout the latter part of the 20th century, were used by both Iraq and Iran to destabilize neighboring governments. It is perhaps a critical element of the Kurdish tragedy that their dependence on

Ayatollah Ruhollah Khomeini, 1979

In January 1979, the government of Iran was toppled by a revolutionary movement led by an Islamic cleric, Ayatolloh Khomeini. The Kurds were quick to join with this revolutionary movement in hopes that this radical change might lead to an independent Kurdistan. But this hope was frustrated when the Islamic community posed its own plan—an Islamic state across all national boundaries.

unreliable allies leaves them open to the charge of treason and subject to even greater oppression when their allies abandon them.

When the Iran-Iraq War finally ended, after eight brutal years, the armed Kurds were left with a dilemma—continue to fight for their own state, fighting now against both Iranian and Iraqi armies, or concede defeat?

Most chose to return home. Those Kurds returning to the Iraqi side of the border would soon face the wrath of Saddam Hussein and his campaign to permanently eliminate the Kurdish "problem." For the Kurds living in Iran, the end of the war brought about a set of unprecedented economic hardships. The Kurdish areas were ill-equipped to accommodate the vast numbers of Iraqi Kurds who had come flooding across the border as the war drew to a close. The war had crippled Iran's economy. Young Kurds flooded into the oil towns or into Tehran in search of work. Jobs were scarce, and the living conditions quickly became horrendous.

The slum-like conditions, the concentration of disaffected young men in urban areas with few prospects and little possibility of earning a living might be a fertile ground for a brand-new Kurdish rebellion to spring up. But no leader was strong enough to capitalize on the opportunity, nor was the Iranian government weak enough to allow it to happen. With the death of the Ayatollah, the conservative forces in charge of Iran continued to shape an authoritative and state-run government. The new president, Hashemi Rafsanjani, expressed some interest in resolving the Kurdish question, but little concrete action was taken.

To many, the core of the conflict between Iran and the Kurds lies in the way the Kurdish movement is defined. To fundamentalist Islamic officials, the Kurds represent a secular (non-religious) group fighting against the rules and regulations imposed by Islamic law. To the Kurds, the debate can not be so simply defined as secular vs. religious or Sunni vs. Shi'ite. Instead, the Kurds claim, they are not fighting against the government's right to impose Islamic law, but instead on the government's right to appoint the judges who decide legal issues. The Kurds, as part of their campaign for self-government, want the right to choose the men who will make and carry out the laws, regardless of what those laws might be.

Jalal Talabani, 2002

Talabani was the leader of the PUK (Patriotic Union of Kurdistan), a left-wing Kurdish group. Talabani recognized that the Gulf War offered an opportunity to ally with the United States against Iraq in exchange for expected American support for the Kurdish cause. But in the end, that support was not forthcoming and the Kurds faced the Iraqi military might on their own.

6

Beyond the Gulf War

1 n August 1990, the Iraqi armies under Saddam Hussein's
direction invaded the kingdom of Kuwait. The unexpected
invasion caused a crisis in the Gulf. U.S. troops soon landed
in Saudi Arabia, in part to prevent the invasion of that country. A
coalition army of some 29 different allies was quickly assembled, but
Saddam Hussein refused to withdraw.

As it became clear that war was a real possibility, the Kurds determined to once more strike out for their own freedom. The leader of the
PUK (Patriotic Union of Kurdistan), a left-wing Kurdish group, was
Jalal Talabani. He understood the opportunity the conflict presented,
and hurried to Washington to attempt to negotiate a deal. His offer:
to organize the Iraqi Kurds to launch an offensive against Saddam

Hussein in return for American support. But his offer was rejected by both the CIA and the U.S. State Department. As a result, the Kurdish groups in northern Iraq remained somewhat outside the fray, participating in the Gulf conflict in limited numbers as members of the Iraqi armed forces.

On January 16, 1991, the Allied armies launched an air campaign, targeting Iraq, followed on February 24 by attacks from ground troops. Iraq was quickly defeated, and a cease-fire was announced on March 3. The event had dealt a serious blow to the Iraqi government, and the Kurds determined to take advantage of the suddenly and unexpectedly weakened central government. An uprising began in more remote regions, with small towns and villages suddenly being seized by Kurdish groups, defining themselves as *pesh merga* (the traditional name for Kurdish guerrillas, meaning "those who are willing to face death"). The demoralized army was caught by surprise and, particularly in areas that lacked a strong military presence, the rebellion was successful. It had not been formally organized, nor even for the most part planned out ahead of time by any Kurdish leadership; it simply resulted from the chaos surrounding the end of the Gulf War.

The Kurds initially caught Saddam Hussein by surprise, and in the first few weeks of March the pesh mergas were able to capture many of the major cities in Iraqi Kurdistan, including Arbil, Sulaymaniya, Jalula, Dohuk, Zakho and Kirkuk. But the element of surprise did not last long. By the third week of March, Saddam Hussein had ordered troops, aircraft, tanks and guns to the northern Kurdish areas to wipe out the rebellion and punish the rebels.

ABSENT ALLIES

The Kurds had believed that the Allied forces would assist them in their efforts to topple Saddam Hussein's regime. Then-U.S. president, George Bush, had called upon the Iraqi people to rise up and overthrow Saddam Hussein's dictatorship. The Kurds believed that they were, in a sense, continuing the Allied offensive against the government in Baghdad and that the Allied forces would come to their aid or, at the least, continue to engage the Iraqi army along the Kuwaiti border to permit the Kurdish forces to seize and hold territory in Kurdistan. Tragically, they were mistaken.

There were a number of reasons why the United States chose not to continue the war, nor to intervene when Saddam turned his troops and headed north to stamp out the Kurdish rebellion. One of the overriding principles that had rallied the allied coalition together was Saddam's flagrant violation of the territorial integrity of another nation. The United States felt it would be contradictory for American forces to then intervene in the internal, domestic affairs of Iraq. The goal of the coalition had been to force Iraqi troops out of Kuwait, not to force Saddam Hussein out of power. The former goal was clear and clearly supported by the international community; the latter would not be. Finally, the United States had no interest in alienating the governments of countries like Turkey and Syria, with Kurdish populations of their own, by seeming to encourage a Kurdish uprising in Iraq.

The pesh merga rebellion had enjoyed success because of the limited presence of police and soldiers able to restrain the crowds, not due to any significant presence of weapons. When the Iraqi tanks rolled into Kurdish territory, when helicopters swooped down and the full fighting force of Saddam's military turned its attention north, the Kurds could put up little resistance. Outnumbered and severely underarmed, they were little match for the Iraqi military.

Saddam had selected as his Minister of Defense General Kamel Hassan, a military commander who had been heavily involved in the brutal Anfal operations against the Kurds in the late 1980s. The General quickly regained all major Kurdish cities, meeting limited resistance. It was becoming clear to the Kurds that the Allied forces had abandoned them. They were on their own.

Panic quickly ensued. The Kurds, who had suffered so tragically in the Anfal operations, remembered full well the brutality of the Iraqi forces and feared that, once more, chemical weapons would begin raining down upon them. Hundreds of thousands of Kurds fled to the Turkish and Iranian borders. The roads were filled with huge masses of people, desperately trying to get out of their country.

The mountains were still cold, and many of the refugees froze to death in a futile effort to escape the Iraqi forces. Estimates vary, but most reports indicate that between 1.5 and 2 million Kurdish refugees attempted to escape— two-thirds of them heading into Iran and approximately 600,000 crossing the Turkish border.

The televised images of women and children desper- ately attempting to cross the mountains in frigid late-winter conditions made for horrifying viewing, and world opinion soon caused a major shift in the perspective on the Kurdish crisis. The United Nations finally addressed the crisis on April 5, passing a resolution (UN Resolution 688) that spelled out its need to intervene. The language is unusual, indicating that the UN felt compelled to take action not because of the human rights abuses committed against the Kurds but instead because of the large numbers of refugees fleeing to other countries.

Ultimately, the West was forced to intervene. A coali- tion was formed to set up a "safe haven" in Iraq's northern region, and President Bush issued an order compelling Iraq to withdraw all of its troops to a spot south of the 36th Parallel (a line south of Mosul and Arbil, but not including the oil-producing area around Kirkuk). Coalition troops moved into the region, and Allied aircraft patrolled the

Iraqi Kurds, 1991

Thousands of Iraqi Kurds were displaced from their homes in northern Iraq following a failed rebellion against Saddam Hussein in 1981. The Kurdish family in this photograph carry their few belongings to a refugee resettlement camp near Zakho, Iran.

skies above the restricted territory, which soon became labeled a "no-fly zone." Some Kurds, reassured by the presence of Allied troops ensuring their safety, returned to their home regions, but many more remained along the borders of Turkey and Iran, seeking asylum.

A LEGACY IN LIMBO

The tragic history of the Kurds continues to this day, as they remain unwanted minorities scattered throughout the Middle East. Their fate continues to be uncertain, heavily dependent on the actions and policies of other countries. Their greatest distinction remains the constancy of their status as a repressed minority, numbering somewhere between 20 to 25 million, and scattered throughout Turkey, Iran, Iraq and, to a lesser extent, Syria.

The Kurds periodically come to the world's attention, either as victims of some civil campaign verging on genocide, or as potential pawns in international disputes or efforts to topple regimes. They then slip back into the shadows of international opinion.

Roughly three-quarters of a century ago, the Treaty of Sèvres promised the Kurds a homeland, a safe region where they could live peacefully and govern themselves. That promise has never been fulfilled and, in a global community that has long moved past the mandates of the First World War, it has largely been forgotten. But to the Kurds, the promise remains alive, a source of hope to a population concentrated in poverty-stricken areas, victimized by unfriendly regimes, resorting to terrorism and guerrilla activities as their only possible resource.

What does the future hold for the Kurds? Is there a possibility that the mandates of the Treaty of Sèvres might one day become reality? (See Appendix: The Treaty of Sèvres)

PROSPECTS IN TURKEY

The most oppressive phase of the Turkish campaign against the Kurds seems to have passed. Turkey is eager to join the European Union—its brutal campaign against the Kurds has been one of the major obstacles to this critical goal. It is eager to cement ties with the West, to continue to play a strategic role within NATO and the world community, but human rights violations continue to haunt a government anxious to move beyond the decades-old conflict with Kurdish freedom fighters.

The PKK continues to fight—in the eyes of the Kurds, this is a campaign to win autonomy; in the eyes of the Turks, their activities are simple terrorism. Targeting

Turkish Kurds, 2001

Kurdish demonstrators chant slogans and flash victory signs during the spring festival celebrations in Istanbul, Turkey. More than 50,000 Kurds marked the Kurdish New Year, but clashes and a ban on such festivities in Istanbul marred the celebration.

tourist sites within Turkey and important Turkish sites, such as embassies and consulates, around the world, the PKK has consistently proved that even the most violent repercussions against the Kurdish community will not snuff out this war.

The Turkish army continues to patrol Kurdish regions, continuing their efforts to "maintain the peace" in this tense territory. Certain liberalizations have occurred, most notably the relaxing of rules preventing Kurds from speaking Kurdish, but this remains the only significant achievement following decades of fighting. Turkey continues to be determined not to allow the formation of a Kurdish state, and it enjoys a strategic partnership with the United States that will provide pressure on American forces to avoid any efforts to assist the Kurdish communities in any nation.

The tragedy is that both sides have lost much and gained little following the decades of civil war. The Kurds have failed to win their own territory, but the Turks have also failed in their goals of compelling all residents of Turkey to proudly define themselves as Turkish. If anything, their brutal oppression, the continued military presence, has guaranteed that the Kurds will see themselves as a minority, isolated and separated from the rest of Turkey. They cannot forget that they are Kurds, because their status is so clearly inferior to the rest of their countrymen.

PROSPECTS IN IRAQ

Resistance continues among the Kurds to the brutal regime of Saddam Hussein, but it is scattered and not unified. Various Kurdish factions, including the KDP and the PUK, attempted to negotiate with Saddam Hussein's government following the end of the Gulf War and the Kurdish uprising that followed. While they were able to achieve a kind of status quo in the Kurdish regions—the so-called safe havens in the north—their accomplishments have been hampered by inter-Kurdish squabbling as the different groups compete for influence over the same territory. Opposition groups did form yet another entity, the Iraqi Democratic Alliance, but this is viewed chiefly as a front for U.S. efforts to destabilize Saddam Hussein's government and as a result is struggling to receive any support from other neighboring nations.

The region remains heavily dependent on international aid. The economy is struggling, as it is throughout Iraq, but in the Kurdish territories the poverty is particularly striking. The community's very existence seems precarious, dependent as it is on the continued efforts of the international community to ensure that the Iraqi government does not turn, once more, against its Kurdish citizens.

A deterrent force of Allied troops (mainly U.S. and Turkish) was stationed in Turkey to ensure the continued safety of the Kurds, as a response to the refugee crisis following the Gulf War. Known as "Operation Poised Hammer," the force seemed a clear sign that the fate of the Kurds in Iraq was highly uncertain. For now, all sides seem to be simply waiting—waiting for another conflict that seems sadly predictable.

PROSPECTS IN IRAN

The most recent policy of Iran toward the Kurds has been the determined elimination of its political structure while allowing the population to drift, unorganized and leaderless. In the latter part of the 20th century, the Iranian government took steps to bomb any KDPI positions inside Iraq that threatened the Iranian frontier. The leader of the KDPI, A.R. Ghassemlou, was assassinated in Vienna on July 13, 1989, while attempting to negotiate with the Iranian government to bring about a non-military solution to the

Kurdish problem. Later investigations made it clear that Iranian diplomats were involved in the assassination.

The Kurdish regions within Iran remain backward and undeveloped. The population is growing rapidly (nearly twice that of the rest of the country) but there are few opportunities, little education, and poor health care. The conditions are ripe for a large population of disaffected young people to rise up against the government, but thus far no strong leader or political power has been able to unify them, and the Islamic regime has been brutally effective in cracking down on any signs of rebellion.

A UNIFIED KURDISTAN

One of the final tragedies of the Kurds is that the goal they still struggle for—a nation of their own—is diminishing in a global community increasingly focusing on international coalitions and pan-national forces. The boundaries of a single state or a single border no longer define a region or its people. New bonds, forged by coalitions, technology, and religious beliefs, are drawing people together in new groupings, and yet the Kurds continue to struggle for the same goal they had more than 80 years ago.

The global community has drastically changed since the long-ago days when the Treaty of Sèvres was first signed. The Ottoman Empire crumbled and vanished. The new state of Turkey arose from its ashes. Iraq fought off colonial influences and attempted to redefine its borders. Iran over-threw a monarchy and refashioned itself into an Islamic republic. American interests shifted from Iran to Turkey, affecting the treatment of Kurds throughout the region.

With each new decade, with each shift in international alliances and interests, the Kurds continue to hope that change will at last bring an independent Kurdistan. The Kurdish claim—that they are really one people, trapped within the borders of other nations—no longer seems realistic. The PKK in Turkey and the Kurds in Iraq seem to have little in common. The conflict among Kurds within Iraq itself makes Kurdish unity unlikely even on a small scale, and virtually impossible across borders. The Kurds remain a victim of history, a footnote in the creation of the modern Middle East.

Gallery of Photographs
from the Kurds

Kurd Porters, Mount Ararat, c. 1893-94

Mount Ararat is in extreme eastern Turkey. Traditionally, Mount Ararat is associated with the mountain on which Noah's Ark came to rest at the end of the Flood as described in the Book of Genesis.

Kalak, c. 1902

This is a photograph of a *kalak* along the Murat River in eastern Turkey. The kalak, a timber raft supported on inflated goatskins, could carry loads of several tons. The goatskins were inflated by using hand bellows.

Ellsworth Huntington (1876-1947) is photographed in the center. Note the American flag. Huntington was a noted American geographer who explored the Tigris River in eastern Turkey.

Armenian Soldiers, Eastern Turkey, c. 1906-09

Almost every major point involving Armenian-Turkish-Kurd relations is disputed.

In 1890, about 2.5 million Christian Armenians lived within the Ottoman Empire—about 1.5 million of these people lived in eastern Anatolia. These Armenians, mostly peasants, lived in areas dominated by Turks and Kurds—in no province did they constitute either a majority or a plurality. There were Armenian communities in most Anatolian towns and in Constantinople itself.

The Armenians, encouraged by Russia, began promoting Armenian territorial autonomy in eastern Anatolia. The resulting persecutions carried out by Turkish troops and Kurdish tribesmen killed thousands of Armenians (1894-96). For the next two decades, the carnage between these peoples continued. The lack of death records makes a final figure impossible.

Kurds, East of the Tigris River, c. 1906-09

This photograph was taken by Bertram Dickson, British Military Consul at Van. In December 1909, Dickson spoke about his travels through Kurdistan before the Royal Geographical Society. A longer, written version of his trip, including a detailed map of the area, appears in *The Geographical Journal*, April 1910 issue. This article ranks among the seminal descriptions of Kurdistan between 1906-09.

Kurdish Sowars, Persia, c. 1908-09

A *sowar* is a mounted ethnic soldier. The Persian government used Kurdish soldiers to police Kurdish areas within the Empire.

During 1908-09, the power of Qajar shah was declining. Persia, later called Iran, was the scene of rival intrigues by pro-British and pro-German groups. Although several million Kurds lived within the western part of the Persian empire, control from Tehran virtually had ceased.

Camel Caravan, 1912

This camel caravan is bringing oil from the Caucasus region of Russia through the Kurdish Azerbaijan to Persia (Iran). The oil is in containers made from animal skins and then secured to the camel in wooden crates.

Kurdish Father and Children, Isfahan Valley, Persia, c. 1912

The Kurdish father, upper right, is photographed with his three children. In traditional Kurdish society, males usually marry at age 20 and females at age 12.

This photograph was taken by Sir Percy M. Sykes (1867-1945). Sykes wrote a two-volume *History of Persia* (1915). He received numerous awards from the Royal Geographical Society. In describing his travels through Persian Kurdistan, Sykes noted: "Guides and escorts are another serious consideration; the former are usually difficult to find, and seldom know the names of any villages or places away from their own."

Kurdish Musicians, Isfahan Valley, Persia, c. 1912

"Kurdish Robber Chiefs," 1912

Morgan Philips Price (1885-1973) gave this photograph its title. Price traveled through Kurdistan in 1912.

Price later reported events of World War I (1914-1918) from Russia for the *Manchester Guardian*. In 1921, he wrote *My Reminiscences of the Russian Revolution,* an account that is sympathetic to the government established by Vladimir Lenin and the Bolsheviks.

Street Scene, Tabriz, 1912

Tabriz was the regional capital of Persian Azerbaijan.

During World War I (1914-1918), the Kurdish population of Tabriz attempted to join the city to other Kurdish enclaves in the Azerbaijan area. Turkish troops defeated this autonomy movement. Then, during the ensuing political chaos in this area, Azerbaijan Kurds did form a self-governing state for about two years (1923-1925). The Kurdish governing body established Kurdish schools with the directive that all males be taught to read and write. In 1925, Soviet troops put down this "revolution."

Kurdish Village, 1913

This photograph is a typical Kurdish village in northwestern Azerbaijan. The structures are made from sun-dried mud and stone.

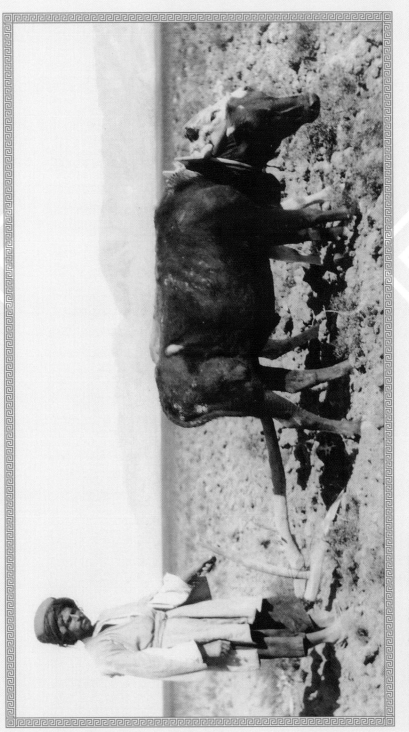

Persian Kurd Plowing, c. 1920-21

The traditional Kurdish way of life was nomadic. However, the enforcement of national boundaries after World War I, forced most Kurds to settle in villages and to farm the land.

On August 10, 1920, the Allied forces that had secured victory in World War I signed a treaty that was intended to decide the fate of the Middle East. The Treaty of Sèvres, named for the location of the meeting, contained 433 separate points, or articles. Three of these dealt specifically with the Kurds:

ARTICLE 62

A Commission sitting at Constantinople and composed of three members appointed by the British, French and Italian Governments respectively shall draft within six months from the coming into force of the present Treaty a scheme of local autonomy for the predominantly Kurdish areas lying east of the Euphrates, south of the southern boundary of Armenia as it may be hereafter determined, and north of the frontier of Turkey with Syria and Mesopotamia, as defined in Article 27, II. (2) and (3). If unanimity cannot be secured on any question, it will be referred by the members of the Commission to their respective Governments. The scheme shall contain full safeguards for the protection of the Assyro-Chaldeans and other racial or religious minorities within these areas, and with this object a Commission composed of British, French, Italian, Persian and Kurdish representatives shall visit the spot to examine and decide what rectifications, if any, should be made to the Turkish frontier where, under the provisions of the present Treaty, that frontier coincides with that of Persia.

ARTICLE 63

The Turkish Government hereby agrees to accept and execute the decisions of both the Commissions mentioned in Article 62 within three months from their communication to the said Government.

ARTICLE 64

If within one year from the coming into force of the present Treaty the Kurdish peoples within the areas defined in Article 62 shall address themselves to the Council of the League of Nations in such a manner as to show that a majority of the population of these areas desires independence from Turkey, and if the Council then considers that these peoples are capable of such independence and recommends that it should be granted to them, Turkey hereby agrees to execute such a recommendation, and to renounce all rights and title over these areas.

The detailed provisions for such renunciation will form the subject of a separate agreement between the Principal Allied Powers and turkey.

If and when such renunciation takes place, no objection will be raised by the Principal Allied Powers to the voluntary adhesion to such an independent Kurdish State of the Kurds inhabiting that part of Kurdistan which has been hitherto been included in the Mosul Vilayet.

[Source: David McDowall, *A Modern History of the Kurds*, New York: I.B. Tauris, 1996, pp. 450-451]

1920 The Treaty of Sèvres is signed, promising the Kurds their own state on Kurdish territory.

1923 Treaty of Lausanne is signed, and much of Kurdistan is granted to the new state of Turkey led by Mustafa Kemal (Atatürk).

1924 Turkey bans all Kurdish schools, organizations, and publications.

1930 The leader of the Kurdish revolt against the Iranian government (Simko) is assassinated during talks with Iranian officials.

1943–45 Kurds, under the leadership of Mustafa Barzani, revolt in Iraq. Barzani ultimately must flee to Iran.

1946 The first Kurdish republic is proclaimed at Mahabad in Iranian Kurdistan. It will last only one year.

1953 A CIA-sponsored coup restores the Shah of Iran to power.

1958 The Iraqi monarchy is overthrown by a military coup led by General Qasim.

1961 Kurdish publications in Iraq are closed; Kurdish armed struggle for liberation begins.

1963 Ba'th Party seizes power in Iraq; Iraqi Army launches new attack against Kurds.

1970 Iraqi government grants Kurds self-rule and language rights; agreement breaks down over control of oil.

1974 Fighting between Iraqi military and Kurds intensifies; thousands of refugees flee to Iran.

1978 Abdullah Ocalan establishes the Kurdish Workers' Party (PKK) in Turkey.

1979 Shah of Iran is overthrown. Ayatollah Khomeini authorizies attacks on Kurds. Barzani dies in the U.S.

1984 Ocalan's PKK begins armed struggle against Turkish military.

1987 First confirmed use of chemical weapons against Kurds by Iraqi government.

1990 Saddam Hussein invades Kuwait.

1991 Kurdish uprising in northern Iraq is violently put down. Nearly two million Kurds flee Iraq. UN condemns Iraq's human rights violations. Turkey launches military attack on PKK bases inside Iraq.

1999 Two rival Iraqi Kurdish factions attempt to negotiate a deal with Iraqi government, designed to reunited Kurdish territory with a more democratic form of government.

BOOKS

Chaliand, Gerard. (ed.) *A People Without a Country*. New York: Olive Branch Press, 1993.

Ciment, James. *The Kurds: State and Minority in Turkey, Iraq, and Iran*. New York: Facts on File, Inc., 1996.

Gunter, Michael M. *The Kurds of Iraq*. New York: St. Martin's Press, 1992

Makiya, Kanan. *Cruelty and Silence*. New York: W.W. Norton & Co., 1993.

McDowall, David. *The Kurds: A Nation Denied*. London: Minority Rights Group, 1992.

O'Ballance, Edgar. *The Kurdish Struggle.* New York: St. Martin's Press, Inc., 1996.

ON THE INTERNET

www.britannica.com

www.countrywatch.com

www.kurdish.com

www.kurdishobserver.com

www.kurdmedia.com

www.kurdistan.org

www.netiran.com

www.pbs.org/wgbh/pages/frontline/shows/saddam/kurds/

www.state.gov

www.turkey.org

www.washingtonpost.com

BOOKS

Chaliand, Gerard. (ed.) *A People Without a Country*. New York: Olive Branch Press, 1993.

Chaliand, Gerard. *The Kurdish Tragedy*. Atlantic Highlands, NJ: Zed Books, 1994.

Ciment, James. *The Kurds: State and Minority in Turkey, Iraq and Iran*. New York: Facts on File, Inc., 1996.

Gunter, Michael M. *The Kurds of Iraq*. New York: St. Martin's Press, 1992.

Human Rights Watch. *Iraq's Crime of Genocide*. New Haven, CT: Human Rights Watch Books, 1995.

Makiya, Kanan. *Cruelty and Silence*. New York: W.W. Norton & Co., 1993.

McDowall, David. *A Modern History of the Kurds*. New York: I.B. Tauris & Co., 1996.

McDowall, David. *The Kurds: A Nation Denied*. London: Minority Rights Group, 1992.

O'Ballance, Edgar. *The Kurdish Struggle*. New York: St. Martin's Press, Inc., 1996.

INTERNET SOURCES

www.britannica.com

www.countrywatch.com

www.kurdish.com

www.kurdistan.org

www.pbs.org/wgbh/pages/frontline/shows/saddam/kurds/

www.washingtonpost.com

Abd al Qadir, Shaykh, 21
Anfal operations against Kurds, 65-66, 69,
    71, 90-91, 100, 102, 107-108
Atatürk, Mustafa Kemal, 47-50, 52, 54, 55,
    56, 74
Azadi (Freedom), 50, 52

Barzani, Mulla Mustafa, 78-82, 83-85, 86,
    87-88, 96-98
Barzinji, Shaikh Madmud, 76
Ba'th party (Iraq), 85-86, 87-88, 91
Britain
    and fall of Ottoman Empire, 19-21
    and Iran, 94
    and Iraq, 21-23, 28, 74-76, 79-80
    and Kurdistan, 20-23, 28, 71-72, 74-76,
        79-80
Bush, George H. W., 108

Christianity, 40
Committee of Union and Progress
    (C.U.P.), 21, 30, 32-33, 45

Demirel, Sulayman, 66

Faysal, King of Iraq, 76
France
    and fall of Ottoman Empire, 19
    and Kurdistan, 20, 21, 28

Ghassemlou, A.R., 113

Hiwa, 80, 81
Hussein, Saddam
    and future, 112, 113
    and invasion of Kuwait, 105-106
    and murder of Kurds, 65-66, 69, 71,
        90-91, 100, 102, 107-108
    and 1974 Kurdish war, 88
    as president, 90

Iran, 30, 36, 38, 93-100, 102-103, 114
    and Britain, 94
    and flight of Kurds from Iraq to, 100,
        102, 108, 109
    and flight of Kurds from Turkey to, 54
    and future of Kurds in, 113-114
    government action against Kurds in,
        95-96, 98-100, 102-103, 113-114
    history of Kurds in, 94
    and Khomeini, 99-100, 102

Kurdish political parties in, 94-95,
    96, 113
and Kurdish rebellions in, 94-96, 103
Kurdish republic in, 95-96
and Kurdistan, 20, 28
location of Kurds in, 93
and Mohammed Reza Shah, 94, 96-99
and Mulla Mustafa Barzani, 96-98
and oil on Kurdish land in, 93, 96
population of Kurds in, 93-94
and Reza Shah, 94
and Treaty of Sèvres, 94
and United States, 96
and war with Iraq, 65-66, 69, 71, 89-91,
    100, 102
Iran-Iraq War, 65-66, 69, 71, 89-91,
    100, 102
Iraq, 28, 30, 36, 38, 69, 71-91, 114, 115
    and Ba'th party, 85-86, 87-88, 91
    and Britain, 21-23, 28, 74-76, 79-80
    and Communists, 84
    and flight of Kurds from, 66, 71, 100,
        102, 108-109, 113
    and flight of Kurds from Turkey to,
        54, 67
    and future of Kurds in, 112-113
    and government action against Kurds
        in, 65-66, 69, 71, 79, 81, 82, 83-85,
        87-88, 90-91, 100, 102, 107-108
    and Gulf War, 105-106
    history of Kurds in, 71-89
    and Hussein's murder of Kurds, 65-66,
        69, 71, 90-91, 100, 102, 107-108
    and independence, 76
    Kurdish political parties in, 58, 81-83,
        84, 85, 87, 90, 105, 112, 113
    and Kurdish rebellions in, 58, 75-83,
        85-86, 87, 88, 90, 105-109, 112-113
    and Kurdish territories in, 71
    and Kurdistan, 20
    and League of Nations, 76
    and Mulla Mustafa Barzani, 78-82,
        83-85, 86, 87-88, 96-98
    and oil on Kurdish land in, 21, 28,
        71-72, 74
    and overthrow of monarchy, 83
    and pesh merga rebellion, 105-109
    and plan for Kurdish state in, 21-23,
        72, 76
    population of Kurds in, 71
    and Qasim, 83-85, 86

and revolt against Qasim, 84
and search for Kurdish leader, 21-23, 25, 72
and Treaty of Lausanne, 74
and Treaty of Sèvres, 25-26, 28, 74
and war with Iran, 65-66, 69, 71, 89-91, 100, 102
Islam
    and Kurds, 39-40, 42-43, 45, 48-49
    and Turkey, 48-49, 57, 58
Ismail Agha (Simko), 94

Judaism, 40

Kemal, Mustafa, 47-50
Khomeini, Ayatollah, 99-100, 102
Kurdish Club, 21-22, 32
Kurdish Democratic Party (Iran), 94, 96, 113
Kurdish Democratic Party (Kurdistan Democratic Party) (Iraq), 82-83, 84, 85, 87, 112-113
Kurdish Hope Society, 32
Kurdish Republic, 95-96
Kurdistan
    and Britain, 20-23, 28, 71-72, 74-76, 79-80
    and fall of Ottoman Empire, 19-23, 71-72
    history of, 28. See also Kurds
    and hope for unification, 114-115
    and independence, 33
    and military power and economic significance, 42-43, 45
    as specific region, 38
Kurdistan Democratic Party (KDP) (Iraq), 58
Kurdistan Democratic Party (KDPT) (Turkey), 58
Kurds
    description of, 35, 36
    and different cultures, 38-42
    exile of, 33
    future of, 109-110, 112-115
    history of, 19-20, 28-33, 40-45
    and independence movements, 30, 33, 36, 40-41, 50, 52, 59-67
    and Islam, 39-40, 42-43, 45, 48-49
    and language, 38
    location of, 36, 41-42, 43. See also Iran; Iraq; Syria; Turkey

and nationalism, 21, 30, 32-33
and 1908 revolution, 32-33, 45
and Ottoman Empire, 19-20, 28-33, 43-45
population of, 36, 110
and religion, 39-40, 42-43, 45, 48-49
as tribal society, 40-41, 45, 52
and unified Kurdistan, 114-115
as warriors, 43
Kurmanji language, 38

Lausanne, Treaty of, 47, 48, 74
Law No. 2510 (Turkey), 55
League of Nations, and Kurdistan, 76

Mosul, 21, 28, 71, 74

Ocalan, Abdullah, 59, 60
Oil, 21, 28, 36, 38
    on Kurdish land in Iran, 93, 96
    on Kurdish land in Iraq, 21, 28, 71-72, 74
    and United States, 96
Operation Poised Hammer, 113
Ottoman Empire, 19-20, 28-30
    fall of, 19-20, 28, 31-32, 43-45
    history of, 28-31
    and Kurds, 19-20, 28-33, 43-45
    and 1908 revolution, 21, 32-33, 45
    and Turkey, 47
Ozal, Turgut, 64, 66

Pahlavi, Muhammad Reza Shah, 94, 96-99
Pahlavi, Reza Shah, 94
Pan-Arabism, 77-78, 83, 84
Patriotic Union of Kurdistan (PUK) (Iraq), 90, 105, 112-113
Pesh merga rebellion, 105-108

Qasim, General, 83-85, 86
Qazi Mohammed, 95

Rafsanjani, Hashemi, 102
Rizgari Kur (Kurdish Liberation) (Iraq), 81-82
Russia, and Kurdistan, 20

Saudi Arabia, 30
Sèvres, Treaty of, 25-26, 28, 74, 94, 110, 114
Sharif Pasha, 22

Soviet Union, and Kurdish republic in
Iran, 95
Surani language, 38
Sykes-Picot Agreement, 19-20, 21
Syria, 28, 30, 36
    and flight of Kurds from Iraq to, 71
    and flight of Kurds from Turkey to, 54

Taha, Shaykh, 22-23
Talabani, Jalal, 105
Turkey, 21, 30, 36, 38, 47-67, 114, 115
    and Atatürk, 47-50, 52, 54, 55, 56, 74
    and division of Turkey, 55-56
    and end of caliphate, 48-49
    and end of sultanate, 48
    and flight of Kurds from, 54, 55,
        64-65, 67
    and flight of Kurds from Iraq to, 66,
        71, 108, 109, 113
    formation of, 20-21, 25
    and future of Kurds in, 110, 112
    and government action against Kurds
        in, 52-56, 58-60, 63-65, 66-67, 112
    and Islamic clerics, 57, 58
    Kurdish political parties in, 58, 59-67,
        110, 112

and Kurdish rebellions in, 50, 52-56,
    58-67, 110, 112
loss of Kurdish identity in, 48-49,
    53-56, 59-60, 63-64, 112
and military government, 57-59
and modernization, 48-50, 53-55
and nationhood, 48
and political parties, 58
and Treaty of Lausanne, 47, 48
and Treaty of Sèvres, 25-26, 28
and violence against Kurds in, 52-56
Turkish Hearth Organization, 54-55

United Nations
    and Kurdistan, 82
    and Kurds in Iraq, 108
United States
    and Iran, 96
    and Kurdistan, 20-21
    and Kurds in Iraq, 108

Village Law (Turkey), 63

Workers' Party of Kurdistan (PKK)
    (Turkey), 59-67, 110, 112
World War I, 19

Cover: Royal Geographical Society
Frontispiece: Royal Geographical Society

page:

57:	AP/Wide World Photos	89:	© Francoise de Mulder/Corbis
61:	AP/Wide World Photos	97:	AP/Wide World Photos
65:	© Francoise de Mulder/Corbis	101:	AP/Wide World Photos
70:	AP/Wide World Photos	104:	AP/Wide World Photos
80:	© Bettmann/Corbis	109:	AP/Wide World Photos
86:	© Bettmann/Corbis	111:	AP/Wide World Photos

Unless otherwise credited all photographs in this book © Royal Geographical Society.
No reproduction of images without permission.
Royal Geographical Society
1 Kensington Gore
London SW7 2AR

Unless otherwise credited the photographs in this book are from the Royal Geographical Society Picture Library. Most are being published for the first time.

The Royal Geographical Society Picture Library provides an unrivaled source of over half a million images of the peoples and landscapes from around the globe. Photographs date from the 1840s onwards on a variety of subjects including the British Colonial Empire, deserts, exploration, indigenous peoples, landscapes, remote destinations, and travel.

Photography, beginning with the daguerreotype in 1839, is only marginally younger than the Society, which encouraged its explorers to use the new medium from its earliest days. From the remarkable mid-19th century black-and-white photographs to color transparencies of the late 20th century, the focus of the collection is not the generic stock shot but the portrayal of man's resilience, adaptability and mobility in remote parts of the world.

In organizing this project, we have incurred many debts of gratitude. Our first, though, is to the professional staff of the Picture Library for their generous assistance, especially to Joanna Wright, Picture Library Manager.

HEATHER LEHR WAGNER is a writer and editor. She earned an M.A. in government from the College of William and Mary and a B.A. in political science from Duke University. She is the author of several books for teens on global and family issues. She is also the author of *Iraq* and *Turkey* in the CREATION OF THE MODERN MIDDLE EAST series.

AKBAR S. AHMED holds the Ibn Khaldun Chair of Islamic Studies at the School of International Service of American University. He is actively involved in the study of global Islam and its impact on contemporary society. He is the author of many books on contemporary Islam, including *Discovering Islam: Making Sense of Muslim History and Society,* which was the basis for a six-part television program produced by the BBC called *Living Islam.* Ahmed has been visiting professor and the Stewart Fellow in the Humanities at Princeton University, as well as visiting professor at Harvard University and Cambridge University.